TEACHING SOCIAL SKILLS TO CHILDREN WITH AUTISM USING MINECRAFT®

TEACHING SOCIAL SKILLS TO CHILDREN WITH AUTISM USING MINECRAFT®

A Step by Step Guide

RAELENE DUNDON

Illustrations by Chloe-Amber Scott

NOT AN OFFICIAL MINECRAFT® PRODUCT.
NOT APPROVED BY OR ASSOCIATED WITH MOJANG.

Jessica Kingsley *Publishers*
London and Philadelphia

First published in 2019
by Jessica Kingsley Publishers
73 Collier Street
London N1 9BE, UK
and
400 Market Street, Suite 400
Philadelphia, PA 19106, USA

www.jkp.com

Library of Congress Cataloging in Publication Data
A CIP catalog record for this book is available from the Library of Congress

British Library Cataloguing in Publication Data
A CIP catalogue record for this book is available from the British Library

ISBN 978 1 78592 461 3
eISBN 978 1 78450 838 8

Printed and bound in the United States

The accompanying PDF can be downloaded from
www.jkp.com/voucher using the code ZEATOCA

For Andrew

CONTENTS

Part 3   Resources

ACKNOWLEDGEMENTS

Thank you to my amazing husband and best friend, Andrew Tompkins, for his support, guidance and encouragement. I could not have completed this book without you.

Thank you also to my talented illustrator, Chloe-Amber Scott, who has brought my vision for this book to life with her wonderful images.

A special thank you to Sarah and her gorgeous girls, who introduced me to Minecraft® and planted the seed of an idea to use the game as a theme for a social skills curriculum.

Finally, thank you to all the children and families who have been involved in our social skills groups over the past few years. Your enthusiasm for the programme has encouraged me to write this book and provide the opportunity for many more children to learn about social skills in a fun and engaging way.

INTRODUCTION

Before I introduce you to the social skills and Minecraft® programme in its final form, I want to give you an idea of how the group came to be, and how it has evolved for use as a social skills curriculum for children with autism and other social difficulties.

As a psychologist starting out in my own private practice in Melbourne, Australia, I wanted to run some social skills training for children with autism but was unsure of where to start. I knew that there was a need for social skills groups amongst clients at our practice and in the local community, but deciding on a curriculum and format was daunting, and figuring out when to run a group that would suit most families was hard. I didn't have the capacity to run groups after school during the school term, but running groups during the day wouldn't work for families. A holiday social skills programme seemed like a logical compromise, so I set out to develop a curriculum that would target skills that I knew were common difficulties for my clients.

The idea was that clients would come to the practice for 90 minutes every day for a week in the school holidays, and spend time talking and doing activities designed to support the development of specific social skills. Children would be grouped according to grade level and be limited to children attending mainstream school settings.

The first groups we ran were not based around Minecraft® or any other particular theme. Each session involved introducing a specific social skills topic, practising the skill using role-play and puppets, completing some related worksheets or activities, and playing group games. The groups were a success according to parents and clinicians, but the kids had other ideas. They wanted more time to do fun activities and play, not talk about social skills, and were resistant to coming back for five days in a row. I had seen these types of groups work well when children were attending once a week, but the intensity of the group over five days seemed to be more challenging for children, and we were not as successful at maintaining their interest and motivation to attend.

But how could we make things more appealing and make sure kids were learning and developing their skills at the same time? The answer, of course, was to listen to our families and be open to trying something different.

During a discussion with one of our parents about their two children with autism and their recent interest in a computer game called Minecraft®, it was suggested that a social skills group that was Minecraft® themed would be a great way to get the kids engaged.

After some investigation into what Minecraft® actually was, and how we might be able to use it in a group setting to teach social skills, we set about planning our first Minecraft® social skills group. I really didn't know much about using Minecraft® at that stage, but armed with the basic commands and the knowledge gained from a few 'how to' YouTube videos, I was hopeful that I could bluff my way through. The first group was run in a therapy room at the practice, with four computers set up on tables along one wall, and a small area for the children to sit on the floor during group discussions. Each session ran for 90 minutes and included some discussion around a specific social skills topic, some specific activities using Minecraft® on the computers in pairs, and a worksheet or activity for participants to take home and complete that reinforced the social skills introduced that day. The children particularly liked the Minecraft®-themed visuals used to introduce each social skill and were eager to work on the computers and share their knowledge of Minecraft® with others, which made up for my own lack of knowledge in this area.

This early group, and those that followed in our first year, provided a great opportunity to tailor the group structure and the curriculum to better suit the needs of the children attending, and to explore the different ways that social skills could be supported in this group environment in both structured and unstructured ways. The group structure was expanded to include movement breaks and some offline activities to cater to each individual child's sensory needs and interests. Surprisingly, we sometimes had children attend who were not that into Minecraft® so needed other activities to keep them engaged. The groups also evolved to include opportunities for the children to practise social skills more naturally while they helped each other complete tasks, shared what they had created and discussed how they used Minecraft® outside the group, and during free play in which the children worked together to achieve goals such as 'defeating the Ender Dragon' (more about that later!).

The most notable difference when we initially ran these groups, compared with more traditional social skills curriculae, is the reaction from the children attending. In the past, when we ran un-themed holiday groups, children were often reluctant to attend and participate in activities. But with the Minecraft® programme we created, the children loved coming back each day and were often disappointed when the groups finished at the end of the week. Even more telling is that they keep coming back, asking to attend again the following holidays. And while they still have to learn and practise social skills, they do so in a way that makes it more interesting for them and allows them to connect with other children around their shared interest.

Three years and over 30 groups later, our Minecraft® social skills groups are still the most popular groups we run, and show no signs of slowing down. The programme we have developed is consistently well received by both the participants and their families, and we have had wonderful feedback from schools regarding the changes they have seen in the behaviour of participants, so much so that several schools are now using parts of the group curriculum to support their students.

The success of the Minecraft® groups has also led us to be more creative and adaptable in how we run our groups in general, and has encouraged us to 'think outside the box' with regard to how we can best support our children to develop competence in their social skills. While Minecraft® is still our number one group programme, being in tune with our clients and their interests has resulted in further groups being created with varying themes based on current trends, leading to more and more children accessing support for their social difficulties in a safe, fun and engaging environment.

In this book, I will guide you through what you need to know to run a Minecraft® social skills group at your school or organization, from understanding why social skills are important and learning about the benefits of using Minecraft® with children with autism to teach social skills, to what equipment you will need and how to set up your room effectively. Then I will share with you the lesson plans, activities and handouts I have developed and used over the past few years, so that you have everything you need to run your own Minecraft® social skills group and make it a success.

Happy Minecrafting!

PART 1

SOCIAL SKILLS AND MINECRAFT®

Chapter 1

WHAT ARE SOCIAL SKILLS?

Social skills can be described as the collection of abilities required to successfully and positively engage, interact and communicate with others in both verbal and nonverbal ways. They are skills that we use every day when we are around other people to ensure that we are in tune with how others are feeling and what they might be thinking, as well as assisting us to continually review and adapt our behaviour to meet the challenge of an ever-changing social landscape.

Social skills are thought to begin to develop from birth and continue to evolve throughout childhood and adolescence, and into adulthood. As infants, we naturally tune in to the faces of adults, and learn through interactions with carers that vocalizations, expressions of emotion and gestures have meaning. As we grow, we start to show interest in peers and become more proficient in communicating our needs and seeking out interactions, but it is not until around the age of five years that we develop an understanding that we have different thoughts, feelings and beliefs to others.

In the early school years, our skills continue to develop and become gradually more sophisticated as we learn about ourselves as individual beings, and seek out social connections with peers to feel like we belong. These early years of school form a training ground for understanding and forming friendships, managing conflict with peers, developing conversation skills and learning to regulate our emotions.

As we move into adolescence, our social skills develop even further, and our connections with peers become more complex. We develop a sense of identity by relating to those in our social circles, and build a stronger sense of our thoughts and beliefs which have a greater influence on our choices and behaviour. Through our previous experiences and knowledge gained from others, we also build further skills in adapting to changing social situations, establishing stronger and deeper relationships with others, and altering our behaviour according to where we are and who we are with.

Finally, as adults, we continue to learn to use our social skills in even more varied ways to understand and navigate the complexities of intimate relationships, manage the different expectations and personalities in the workplace, maintain friendships and family connections, and operate effectively in a world reliant on social interaction to ensure we have everything we need to live.

With the dynamic nature of social skills, and the ever-changing social landscape that we live in, it may be that our social skills never really stop developing. Given that we use these skills every day, and throughout our lives, it is not surprising that gaining a better understanding of how social skills develop and why we need them has become the focus of many clinicians and theorists, who are helping to highlight the importance of these skills, and develop ways of supporting individuals who experience difficulties in this area.

Why are social skills so important?

It now seems to be widely accepted that well-developed social skills are essential for more than just making friends and having relationships. Research suggests that along with forming connections with others, competence in social skills is linked to increased academic achievement, future career success, and better mental health.

But what are social skills really? What abilities make up this essential collection of skills and why are they important to so many aspects of our lives?

Social communication

At the core of being social is interacting with others, and to have positive interactions, we must first be able to communicate our wants and needs effectively, and understand the communication of others. To do this, we need to be able to understand and use both verbal and nonverbal cues. This may sound simple but there is a lot involved in communicating that we are often not conscious of, as it seems to happen for most of us almost automatically.

In even the most basic interaction with another person as an adult, we are taking in and interpreting the other person's facial expression, body language, the words they are saying and the tone in which they are saying it, as well as attempting to demonstrate consistent facial expressions and body language ourselves, while formulating an appropriate verbal response. In that same moment we are also considering previous interactions we have had with that person, the context of the current conversation, and the message we are trying to convey. These skills develop throughout childhood to enable us to effectively participate in and make sense of social interactions and have positive social experiences. Using greetings appropriately, maintaining the back-and-forth in a conversation, and knowing how to start and end a conversation are also important social communication skills that assist us to have positive interactions with others, whether they are peers or family members.

For individuals who have difficulties with aspects of social communication, interactions with others can be confusing and anxiety provoking. A child who is not aware of greetings and the rules of conversations may only talk about their own special interests instead of engaging in a back-and-forth dialogue, or not respond to a peer's greetings or attempts to start a conversation, resulting in them being labelled as rude or uninterested. If a child has difficulty recognizing the facial expressions and body language of others, they may miss subtle cues that others are busy or not wanting to play, and then become confused when the peer is annoyed or angry with them for continuing to try to engage them.

Given that we use social communication skills whenever we are in the presence of others, it is easy to see how important these skills are to all aspects of our lives, and how difficult life may be if these skills have not fully developed in line with our peers.

Cooperation

Whenever we work or play with others, at preschool, school, home or in the community, we need skills that enable us to cooperate to achieve a goal or follow a plan. To cooperate effectively we have to be able to tolerate the presence of others in our environment, know how to take turns and share, give and receive help, lead and follow, and work well together. These skills also involve the ability to pay attention to the people we are with and what is happening around us, so we can actively adapt what we are doing to suit the situation and what is needed to achieve a desired outcome.

For some children with social difficulties, even tolerating the presence of another child in close proximity can be a challenge, making cooperating with others an unlikely proposition until support can be provided to manage having others in their environment and having some positive social experiences. For others, the idea of working together with peers is attractive; however, they may need to be fully in control of the play or the plan, leading to conflict when a peer has an idea or wants to do things differently.

Certainly, learning and practising the social skills needed to cooperate throughout childhood is an essential part of social development that becomes even more vital to us as adults in the workplace and in relationships. Without these skills, our ability to work together with others in any capacity would be significantly impaired.

Friendship

The ability to make and maintain friendships is often seen as the ultimate social goal, and has its own unique set of skills associated with it. Friendship is not just about interaction, it is about making a meaningful connection with another person that lasts across time and involves shared experience and enjoyment. Some of the skills considered important for making and maintaining friends include showing empathy, demonstrating interest in others, giving compliments, apologizing, active listening and sharing enjoyment.

Having friends and experiencing a feeling of belonging is often viewed as essential to wellbeing, and has been well documented as being a protective factor against the adverse effects of mental health disorders and social isolation.

Many children with social difficulties want to have friends, but either don't know how to make them or have a lot of trouble keeping them. Some struggle with how to initiate the interactions necessary to begin a friendship (e.g. greetings, asking questions, finding common interests, etc.) while others are able to make those connections to start with but lack the skills and knowledge to maintain the friendship over time (e.g. showing interest in others, having reciprocal conversations, sharing enjoyment). Both of these situations can lead to social rejection and isolation.

With a link between social connection and friendship, and positive mental health well established, providing support to children with deficits in this area may not only support their social development in general but also have a positive impact on their ongoing social and emotional wellbeing throughout their lives.

Social problem solving

It seems to be the nature of interacting with people that there will be times when, either within our social interactions or due to the environment we are in, unexpected or unpredictable things happen. At these times, we need to use our social problem-solving skills to find ways to manage situations effectively. We do this by being flexible in our thinking, considering possible scenarios and outcomes, understanding other people's points of view and compromising. These skills require the use of imagination as a tool to facilitate our ability to be adaptable and flexible, and to look at situations from different perspectives to find appropriate solutions.

Flexible thinking and imagination are often poorly developed in children with social difficulties, making it hard for them to formulate ways to manage challenging situations and solve problems effectively. For example, a child who has difficulty imagining how another child may be feeling in a given situation may act only with their own wants in mind and not understand why their peer becomes upset that the peer's wants are not being considered. Or a child who is very inflexible in their thinking may become distressed when a favourite activity is not available in the classroom and be unable to move on to something different because they cannot imagine any alternative activities or possible solutions to their problem.

Focusing on developing problem-solving skills such as flexibility and imagination is not just beneficial for children in managing social situations, but is also integral to expanding a child's skills in thinking critically and learning.

Self-control

Another essential aspect of social interaction is the ability to effectively manage our own emotions and behaviour, particularly in reaction to others, which is often referred to as self-control. To do this we need to be able to recognize and understand our own emotions, manage our reactions to people or situations that elicit strong feelings, understand how our behaviour impacts others, and have knowledge about what behaviour is expected in different settings and in response to different social scenarios.

Children who struggle with self-control often have difficulty regulating their emotions and behaving appropriately in social situations, particularly when there is conflict or when things don't go as expected. This difficulty can impact on a child's ability to recognize negative emotions in themselves and accept help to calm, or may prevent them from being proactive in using calming or problem-solving strategies to manage a challenging situation effectively. The unpredictable and often volatile nature of self-control difficulties can lead to further social difficulties, including social rejection and isolation, as peers become uncertain or fearful of children who regularly have emotional or aggressive outbursts or act in impulsive ways. For example, a child who cries and throws things whenever he loses a game is likely to alienate himself from peers, as they will see the behaviour as unfair and an overreaction, and lead to them avoiding playing with him due to interactions not being fun.

Self-control is a skill that is essential not just for effective emotional regulation and social interaction in children, but also for the effective management of problems and conflicts across the lifespan. Supporting children to learn these skills early in their development can provide them with the tools they need not just to manage the difficult feelings they will experience in the playground and classroom, but also to set them up to be successful, well-regulated adults.

Competence in social skills provides children with the scaffolding on which many aspects of learning and development can build and grow. Skills in areas such as social communication, cooperation, friendship, problem solving and self-control support children to successfully navigate the social world and build meaningful connections with the people in their lives. By recognizing the importance of social skills in children, and giving them opportunities to develop these skills, we are assisting children to grow into the successful, socially confident adults that we hope they can be.

Chapter 2

HOW ARE SOCIAL SKILLS IMPAIRED IN CHILDREN WITH AUTISM?

Autism spectrum disorder is a neurodevelopmental condition that is characterized by deficits in social communication and interaction, and restricted, repetitive patterns of behaviour, interests and activities. These deficits result in difficulties with using and understanding nonverbal communication, engaging in reciprocal social-emotional interaction and forming social relationships.

But what do these deficits actually look like in children with autism, and why do they occur? While there are many theories that attempt to explain why social skills may be impaired in autistic individuals, there does not appear to be one theory that collectively explains all the difficulties that they experience. Instead, it may be that there are a number of factors that contribute to the presentation of social impairments in children with autism.

Considering the many theories that have been developed about autism in recent years, as well as my many years of experience working with autistic children and adolescents, there are several factors that I believe are likely to contribute to the social difficulties experienced by individuals with autism. These factors are: poor theory of mind; weak central coherence; limited imagination; reduced social experience; and difficulty with learning intuitively.

Poor theory of mind

The term 'theory of mind' refers to the ability to understand that others have thoughts, feelings and beliefs different to your own, and to be able to see things from another person's perspective or 'put yourself in someone else's shoes'. This ability is at the core of many aspects of social competence.

When an individual has well-developed theory of mind, they are able to consider how their words and behaviour may impact others, ensure that others have enough information to understand the context of something they are talking about, and recognize that others may not share the same thoughts and feelings about an issue or situation. This then assists with how a person interacts with the people they are with and the environment they are in. While we are not usually conscious of it, we use theory of mind skills all the time to understand other people's emotions and behaviour, and guide our own words and actions.

Individuals with autism often demonstrate delayed or impaired abilities associated with theory of mind, which can make social interaction difficult. Without appropriate insight into other people's thoughts, feelings and behaviour, or understanding of how their own behaviour impacts others, autistic children and adolescents in particular, can find themselves in situations in which others become upset or angry with them, or seem confused or surprised by their behaviour, and they do not understand what they have said or done wrong.

For example, have you ever had an autistic child approach you and start telling you a detailed story about something, but they appear to have started in the middle and become frustrated when you don't know what they are talking about? It is likely that the child assumed that you knew what they were talking about because they had not yet developed theory of mind and therefore assumed that any knowledge they had, you had too. Or what about the adolescent with autism who laughs when they see a classmate fall over and cut their knee, and then is confused when they are reprimanded for their behaviour? Again, if the adolescent in question does not have good theory of mind, they may assume that because they thought it looked funny, the person who fell would also think it was funny and laugh, rather than understanding that the classmate may be hurt and have different thoughts and feelings about the accident.

Without well-developed theory of mind, children and adolescents with autism can experience ongoing difficulties with engaging in social interaction and forming connections, as their lack of insight into themselves and others can create misunderstanding, confusion and sometimes conflict with others.

Weak central coherence

Central coherence is the term used to describe the ability to take in multiple separate pieces of related information and put them together to make a cohesive whole. In social situations, it involves filtering out relevant from irrelevant information, and making sense of the overall picture or message being communicated by considering verbal and nonverbal cues, and the context in which the interaction occurs.

For many people with autism, there is a tendency to focus on individual details rather than being able to take in the bigger picture, which is considered to be an indication of weak central coherence. While the ability to focus on detail would be considered a strength in many workplaces, getting stuck on detail in social situations can be the cause of considerable difficulties, as important information necessary to engage in a positive social interaction could be missed.

Consider a situation in which an adolescent with weak central coherence sees a friend across the lunch room at school and rushes over excitedly to say 'hello' in a loud voice, without taking in the friend's facial expression and body language and the surrounding context. The friend whispers angrily to the adolescent that it is 'not a good time', leaving the adolescent feeling upset and confused. Now consider the bigger picture – there are several groups of children talking quietly amongst themselves in the lunch room, including the friend of the adolescent in question. The mood in the lunch room is subdued, and it is evident that some of the children have been crying, and others look sad and distressed. Was it appropriate for our adolescent to rush into the room to greet his friend? Taking into account the context, coming in excitedly was not an appropriate way to enter the situation, as it appears that something distressing has occurred. But when you don't pay attention to the context, and just focus on the detail, which in this case was the friend being in the room, it is easy to misread a situation and say or do the wrong thing.

Given that being able to 'read the room' and take in relevant information from social situations is something that many individuals with autism struggle with, it is easy to see how weak central coherence can negatively influence the likelihood of having positive social interactions at home, at school and out in the community.

Limited imagination

When we think of imagination, we often think of a person's ability to be 'creative' and 'artistic'. However, imagination can also be defined as the ability to mentally represent sights, sounds, smells and other sensations without them being physically present. This ability is something that we use every day, not just to make up stories or visualize somewhere we would rather be during a busy day at work, but also to formulate possible solutions to problems, predict what might happen next in social situations, and make smart guesses about other people's thoughts, feelings and actions.

Individuals with autism spectrum disorder often demonstrate difficulties with imagination, particularly with regard to play and social situations. This does not mean people with autism are not creative or have no imagination; what it means is that autistic individuals may have difficulty imagining situations that they haven't experienced before or that involve the thoughts and behaviour of others.

Difficulties with imagination in children with autism may be demonstrated in a variety of ways. A child may not be able to imagine what it will be like to stay at a holiday house for a family holiday, leading to them experiencing high levels of anxiety and distress when the holiday is suggested. Or a child may have been once to a shopping mall and been given a special treat of a cupcake, resulting in them expecting a treat every time they go to the shopping mall as they cannot imagine a different outcome to their visit. With regard to social situations, a child may have learned a script of what to say when greeting someone and what the person is likely to say back, but be unable to respond when the person they are talking to says something unexpected, as they were unable to imagine and plan for other possibilities for the interaction.

As social situations are ever-changing and evolving, having the ability to imagine possibilities and adapt to what others do and say is essential for successful social interactions. With difficulties using imagination to predict the behaviour of others and problem solve in challenging situations, it may be that the need for consistency and predictability demonstrated by children with autism stems in part from an inability to imagine anything different to that which they have experienced or been explicitly taught.

Reduced social experience

When considering the social difficulties that children with autism face, it is also important to take into account the external factors that may influence social impairment. One such factor is the opportunity for positive social experience. For many families, having a child with autism brings with it increased social isolation. Especially when children are young, but often also throughout childhood and adolescence, a child's sensory sensitivities, difficulties with emotional regulation, impaired communication skills and challenging behaviour can lead to negative interactions with peers. Understandably, when these negative interactions are frequent and distressing, parents may become reluctant to take their child out into the community, limiting the child's exposure to social situations and reducing the possibility for positive experiences.

Many of the families I work with recount distressing experiences involving their children with autism that lead them to avoid public outings and other social settings such as children's parties and family events. Incidents such as an autistic child hitting or biting another child at a playground, or having a big meltdown at the supermarket over not being given a treat at the checkout, are unfortunately commonplace for many parents, and can be so embarrassing and emotionally draining that parents choose not to put themselves or their children in those situations again.

Providing parents with the skills and support they need to feel confident to venture out into the community with their child, and giving children with autism social opportunities in supported and structured environments, may assist with the further development of social skills in positive ways.

Ability to learn intuitively

In the social world, there are many unwritten rules that we are expected to know and follow without being told what they are. We learn these rules through watching the social interactions of others and through interacting with peers and learning from our social successes and mistakes.

But what happens when we struggle to learn intuitively from others and from our own experiences? For many children with autism, learning from watching social interactions and reflecting on personal experiences is very difficult, often resulting in them making the same social errors over and over again. While their neurotypical peers generally pick up these skills naturally, and will change their behaviour based on the reactions of others, autistic individuals often require explicit teaching of these skills and rules and an explanation of why their use is necessary, as well as the opportunity to practise before these skills are mastered.

For example, typically developing students in a classroom are usually quick to understand that when the teacher gives them a stern look it means that they are doing something the teacher does not approve of and they need to stop. However, a student with autism may interpret the teacher's facial expression as serious or concentrating, and not realize that they are doing something wrong. Alternatively, a child with autism may not understand that while it is acceptable to eat dinner with his fingers at home, it is not considered good manners when he is eating at a friend's house.

This inability to intuitively understand hidden social rules and learn from the experiences of others can lead to confusion and misunderstandings that may negatively impact in social interactions and experiences.

There are many factors that have been identified as potentially influencing the development and effective use of social skills in children with autism, creating a complex picture of the social deficits that are experienced by autistic individuals. The good news, however, is that there are also many methods we can use to support children with autism. In the coming chapters we will explore how to use one of these methods, social skills groups, to effectively teach social skills to children with autism.

Chapter 3

HOW CAN GROUP PROGRAMMES SUPPORT CHILDREN WITH AUTISM TO DEVELOP SOCIAL SKILLS?

Social skills groups can be an effective part of an intervention plan for children with autism and other social difficulties, providing a unique opportunity to learn and practise social skills with peers in a safe and secure environment.

The use of group programmes to teach social skills to children and adolescents with autism has been widely accepted as an intervention for many years and is considered evidence-based practice. Research regarding the most effective format and structure of group programmes is difficult to find, however, likely due to the many programmes available and the varied content and styles of delivery. In addition, children attending social skills groups often also attend other therapy services and receive support in other ways; associating clear outcomes with attending a social group in isolation is therefore challenging.

What the evidence does tell us is that children who attend social skills groups often demonstrate improvements in social skills in a number of areas including increased social awareness, improved social communication, increased incidences of initiating social interaction with peers, and improved social problem solving. Further, successful groups can be run in schools or clinics or out in the community, and may include only children with autism and other social difficulties or be combined groups with neurotypical peers.

Features of successful group programmes

Over the past several years, I have been lucky enough to run social skills groups both in schools and at our clinic, with children ranging in age from 4 to 12 years, and have seen first-hand the positive impact that social skills groups can have on children with autism and their peers. Through my experience I have learned that some of the most important elements of a successful group programme are ensuring that the children are engaged, that information is tailored to that particular group's needs, and that there is flexibility in how the information is presented.

Engagement

How to attract and hold a child's interest is probably one of the most important considerations of any educator, allied health professional or parent who is charged with helping a child learn. No matter how important the message we are trying to communicate, if we don't grab a child's attention and keep them interested, they will not learn. This is especially evident when trying to teach children something that they find difficult, such as social skills.

I have found that the best ways to keep children engaged in groups are to ensure things are going at a steady pace by not engaging in any one activity for too long, getting the children up and doing things rather than just sitting and talking, using games and sensory breaks to cater to their need for movement, and incorporating special interests where possible to spark their interest and make information more relatable.

Another important element for engagement is to have fun. Using humour and finding your 'silly' side can be a very effective way to help get children engaged and enjoying the group experience, especially for children in preschool and primary school.

Finally, it is extremely important to establish a relationship with each child in your group. If a child feels connected to you, and knows you like them and are interested in them, they are far more likely to engage in the programme. Connecting with a child may be as simple as knowing what their special interest is and asking them about it each session, or sharing some information about yourself that you think they might be interested in knowing. It is also important to be consistent in your behaviour and reactions, and for a child to see that you mean what you say and therefore can be trusted. Brief, positive interactions and consistency can help a child trust and feel safe with you in the group environment, and if they feel safe and comfortable, they are likely to engage and learn more effectively.

Tailoring the material to group needs

While we do not always have comprehensive information about the children attending a group, having an idea of their basic skills and needs is very useful in determining what information will be most beneficial for them to learn throughout a programme.

When using a pre-written curriculum this can be difficult, as there are set topics and activities that need to be covered each session; however, if you are creating the programme yourself, or can choose from a selection of pre-written plans, you can tailor the programme to suit your group's needs.

You might gather information about a child's pre-group skills by using a social skills screening tool. Alternatively, you could introduce some basic principles or concepts in your first group session and gauge whether the group members are already competent in these skills or need to learn or review them before moving on to more complex ideas. For example, if you are running a group that is going to be focusing on friendship skills, it may be important that children in the group already understand facial expressions and body language, and basic conversation skills. If more complex friendship skills are taught before a child has the basic foundations of social communication, they are unlikely to really benefit from the instruction as they do not have the basic knowledge to build on. In this case, time may need to be spent establishing these basic skills before going on to more complex subject matter.

Flexibility with the presentation of information

As with any setting in which children are involved, there are bound to be differences in language abilities, attention and learning within a group, and at times the suggested format for materials may not be suitable for your group members. It is important to be flexible and to 'think outside the box' when it comes to presenting information to ensure the children in your group have the best possible chance to learn and develop their skills. For example, it may be necessary to use visual prompts or props to support understanding of concepts with some children, or to use video clips instead of books to introduce topics and keep the children in your group engaged. Or perhaps some music might be what works for your group best. Being flexible with the delivery of your material means that you can be sure that your group members are engaged, learning, and really benefiting from the group experience.

Benefits of group programmes for children with autism

As we have previously discussed, autism spectrum disorder is a neurodevelopmental condition that is characterized in part by deficits in social skills, resulting in difficulties with social communication and interaction, and impaired abilities to form social relationships. These difficulties with social skills can significantly impact an autistic individual's ability to function at home, at school and out in the community, and acquiring the social understanding and skills necessary for effective social interaction can be extremely challenging. This is where social skills groups come in.

While individuals with autism often have difficulty naturally understanding and developing social skills, with time and practice they can learn the skills they need to be more successful in their social interactions. Social skills groups offer children and adolescents with autism a safe and supported environment in which to learn and practise specific skills. These skills are usually presented using a variety of methods known to be effective in teaching individuals with autism, such as direct teaching, modelling, role-playing/practise, positive reinforcement, and involving parents and carers.

Direct teaching

Direct teaching usually involves an adult providing instruction to a child or adolescent around a specific skill. This may include breaking down the skill into parts, discussing why the skill is important and when it might be used, reflecting on real examples to illustrate the skill in meaningful ways, and using visuals to support understanding and explain the skill in different contexts. Direct teaching is particularly important for children with autism as they often struggle to identify specific skills and understand them in social contexts, leading to misunderstandings and confusion in social settings when it is not clear what is happening, and how they should be reacting.

Modelling

Modelling is a technique that involves the demonstration of a target skill that a child or adolescent can watch and learn from. Modelling can be done by peers, siblings, teachers or other adults, or alternatively can be conducted using toys or puppets. Further, it can be done live, where the child or adolescent watches a skill being demonstrated in person, or it can be done using a pre-recorded video of people, toys or characters, also known as video modelling.

Video modelling can be particularly useful in teaching social skills, as the pre-recorded nature of a video lends itself to be viewed multiple times if required, and to be stopped part way through to provide an explanation or answer questions when needed. It is also relatively simple to find videos to use whether through products designed for teaching social skills, clips from favourite television shows or movies, or videos made yourself that feature peers or adults, or the children attending the groups themselves.

Role-playing/practise

As with any new skill a child is trying to acquire, the more opportunities they have to practise and receive constructive feedback so they continue to improve, the more likely they are to develop, strengthen and use that skill in their everyday lives.

Role-playing involves practising a skill through acting out a specific situation or interaction. Again, as with modelling, this can be done with peers, adults, puppets or toys.

For children who are quite reserved or anxious about acting something out with another person, using puppets can be a nonthreatening way of assisting them to practise a skill. Once they feel more confident, they may be open to practising with a peer or sibling. I have found that role-playing is especially useful as a tool for rehearsing social language and conversation, and can be scripted to support a child to develop their skills or to assist a child to consider how to react when faced with different social scenarios.

Positive reinforcement

Reinforcing appropriate social behaviour can be very useful in providing autistic children and adolescents with motivation and feedback regarding their social skills and encouraging them to keep practising and making attempts at positive social interaction.

Within a group, reinforcement may be in the form of a token system that is used to highlight when a specific skill or skills are used appropriately, leading to a prize at the end of the session. Reinforcement can also be more social in nature, particularly when at school or home, with a quiet word of encouragement or praise to let a child know that you recognize their effort or that they have demonstrated a skill well.

Involving parents and carers

It is also important to remember that no child exists in isolation, and that the short time that a child spends in group is unlikely to result in skills continuing to develop and generalizing to other settings unless support, discussion and practice of the skills occurs outside the group. Ensuring that parents, teachers and caregivers are provided with information about what skills are being targeted in the group and how they can help a child to further develop these skills is very important in supporting the child to maintain and use the skills they have learned over time. This information can be provided in the form of handouts that describe the topic of each session and how parents can help, home tasks that are designed to be completed with the help of parents and that review the information presented in the previous session, and feedback about the child or adolescent's performance throughout the course of the group with suggestions for parents in how to support their child to further develop their skills at home and school.

Additional benefits of group programmes

The benefits of attending a social skills group go beyond the specific training that individuals with autism receive with regard to social skills. The group environment lends itself to many other valuable experiences that can assist children with autism to develop their social abilities and have positive social interactions.

Practising skills with peers in a naturalistic environment

Attending a group programme provides children with autism with the opportunity to practise their skills more naturally with peers. Many children will receive individual social skills instruction from therapists, which can be very helpful in building understanding of social interaction and social competence. However, practising these skills only with adults does not allow individuals to experience more typical social interaction with same-age peers. A group setting gives children the chance to interact more naturally with others, with feedback and the support of adults available when needed to assist them to further develop their skills.

Meeting children who have similar challenges to themselves

For many children and adolescents with autism, whether or not they are aware of their diagnosis, it can feel as though they are alone in the challenges they face with social interaction day to day. Coming to a group where they have the opportunity to meet peers who experience the same kinds of challenges that they do can help give them a feeling that they are not on their own and provide them with a sense of belonging. Further, this feeling of belonging can contribute positively to a child's self-esteem and self-confidence, supporting a more positive overall view of themselves.

Possibility of forming friendships that extend outside the group

In environments such as the classroom and playground, it can be hard for children and adolescents with autism to initiate and maintain social interactions with peers. This can further lead to problems developing friendships, as the opportunity to spend time getting to know classmates and connecting with them is limited.

When children participate in social skills groups, the small number of children along with adult facilitation provides an environment where connection with peers is supported and certainly encouraged. This gives children the chance to find others who like the same things and enjoy completing activities together, which in my experience often results in children arranging to meet up and spend time with each other outside of the group.

For children and adolescents with autism, receiving support to better understand and appropriately use a range of social skills is an essential part of any intervention programme. Social skills groups can provide autistic individuals with the assistance they need to effectively learn about and practise social skills in a safe and supportive environment.

Chapter 4

WHAT IS MINECRAFT®?

Minecraft® is certainly not your average video game. Since its release in 2011, it has grown in popularity to become a worldwide phenomenon with over 55 million active monthly global users, and it shows no signs of slowing down. Minecraft® is available on an increasing number of game platforms, including PC/Mac, iPad, Xbox 360 and Nintendo Switch, and an update in 2017 enables players on different devices to play in the same worlds (the 'better together' update), making it possible for friends and family members to play together across platforms.

So why is a simple video game so popular? Minecraft® has been described as 'digital LEGO®', as its open platform and 'sandbox' quality gives players the ability to do and build just about anything. The term 'sandbox' refers to the fact that players can virtually start with a blank canvas and create their own worlds and experiences, using building blocks, resources from the land and their own creativity. Players can choose to play in 'survival' mode in which minerals must be mined, food grown and creatures defeated as part of an open adventure, or in 'creative' mode in which they are free to make things with unlimited resources. It is a first-person player game, meaning that the player interacts directly with the game environment from their point of view, and can be played as an individual, or in a multiplayer option allowing for play with others on thousands of online servers.

The beauty of Minecraft® seems to be its simplicity. In a 3-D world of basic blocks and simple commands, virtually anything is possible. This simplicity also lends itself to creativity, flexibility and problem solving, which are important elements of learning. The learning and teaching potential of Minecraft® has been recognized by its creator, Mojang, in the development of MinecraftEdu® – a specific platform designed to enable educators to use Minecraft® as a teaching tool in the classroom with administrative support and resources created and shared by users. MinecraftEdu® is currently used in thousands of schools worldwide to teach subjects from art and history to science and maths, with new and innovative ways of using the platform being developed all the time.

How do you play Minecraft®?

The basic premise of Minecraft® really is straightforward. The world is made up of blocks or cubes that can be used to build all kinds of structures, or can be mined for materials that are needed to make or 'craft' useful items such as weapons or tools.

The game can be as complex or basic as the player wants. For example, a single player in creative mode has access to an endless supply of blocks and items and can make and do almost anything they want without being bothered by monsters or limited by materials. In contrast, a player in survival mode on a multiplayer server must mine for materials and hunt for food, while protecting themselves from monsters and other players.

Further, in survival mode a player can be killed by monsters, other players, or materials such as lava, and although they can respawn back into the game they will lose any items and materials they have gathered, having to start from scratch again. Playing in survival mode therefore becomes a game of strategy and planning, in which storing or hiding materials just in case you respawn is necessary, and collecting weapons and protecting yourself is essential.

For more advanced users there are even more possibilities within the gameplay, including crafting complex items, taming animals, farming, trading with Villagers, using enchantments and potions to attribute special qualities to weapons or give players special powers (e.g. night vision), and building automated machines and devices using Redstone (the Minecraft® equivalent of electricity).

Controls

The different platforms used to play Minecraft® all have different controls for movement; however, the way players move through the game is the same. Regardless of the platform, both the player's left and right hands are utilized, as one hand controls point of view, orientation and hand movements within the game (e.g. pick up, put down, break, hit, etc.), and the other hand controls direction and type of movement within the world (forward, back, left, right, jump, fly, etc.). Other controls for functions such as checking inventory and crafting materials are usually available through additional menus or buttons specific to each platform.

For example, when playing Minecraft® on the Mac or PC, players utilize both the mouse and keyboard to navigate throughout the game. On the keyboard, the letter keys W, A, S and D are used to move the player forward, left, back and right, respectively, while the mouse controls the direction your character is facing. The space bar is used to make the player jump or fly. The left shift key allows a player to descend from flight in a controlled way, or disembark from a boat or minecart, and the letter E key provides access to the player's inventory. As well as the mouse being used to control the character's point of view, the mouse left click controls hitting or breaking objects, and the right click controls the placement of objects and opening of doors, and also allows a player to get into a minecart or boat, or mount an animal (e.g. horse, pig) to ride it.

Worlds

There are a number of different options available to Minecraft® players with regard to the worlds that they play in. Minecraft® has infinite worlds, and can randomly create a new one every time you play if that's what you choose. Alternatively, you can find a world and make it your own, and even invite friends to join you in the game.

As I mentioned previously, the main world options are single or multiplayer. Single player provides you with a world that you are in completely on your own, while multiplayer places you in a world where other users are also playing and can connect with you. There are benefits and drawbacks to each kind of play. Single player mode allows you to play without having to be concerned about other players attacking you or trying to take your things, but is not ideal if you want to play and build with a friend. Multiplayer allows you to play with others and interact with them online, but in doing so allows people you don't know to chat to you and possibly 'grief' you (i.e. deliberately annoy and frustrate you by repeatedly destroying your things and getting in your way).

An alternative option to using a public world is to create your own Minecraft® server and share the details with friends to allow access only to those who you know and want to play with. This can be done by downloading Minecraft® server software and installing this on your computer or game console – which can be quite complicated if you are not tech savvy – or by signing up to Minecraft® Realms. Realms allows you to have your own private server with up to three different worlds in it, and you choose who else is able to join by sending invitations to specific players. This avoids the problem of having unknown and unwanted people in your world, while still allowing you to play with friends. For the groups we run at my psychology practice, we use Minecraft® Realms to ensure that everyone can play safely and we are in control of the world and what is in it. This also allows us to change the world and its appearance to suit the activities that are going to be completed each session.

Blocks

Minecraft® wouldn't have its unique and iconic look without the blocks that make up almost everything in the game, from the landscape and buildings to the characters themselves.

The most basic of the blocks would probably be dirt blocks, which cover much of the surface of any Minecraft® world and are easily broken. Other blocks vary in strength and availability, with some being commonly found in the landscape, such as stone, wood and sand, and others being rare and often only found if they are mined from underneath many layers of dirt or bedrock, such as diamond, gold and iron. Of course, when in creative mode, a player has simple and immediate access to all block types through their inventory, but in survival mode different blocks need to be mined and collected.

To create complex items such as weapons and tools, blocks need to be combined or crafted using a 'crafting table', which is a special block that can be collected from a player's inventory or made using wooden planks. Once players have access to a crafting table, they can create a seemingly endless array of weapons, tools and objects from raw materials using recipes that combine the materials in specific ways. For example, to create an iron sword, the recipe requires two iron ingots (made from iron ore) and a wooden stick.

In addition to crafting, blocks also have another important role in gameplay – building. Players can create anything from simple houses or shelters out of wood, to complex and extravagant castles, and anything in between. Blocks are also often used by players to create 'pixel art' or replicate real-life structures or pieces of artwork such as the Mona Lisa or the Eiffel Tower.

Biomes

In the Minecraft® universe, each world can contain any number of biomes or environments, each with their own unique climate, flora and fauna, and geographical features. These biomes create regions within a Minecraft® world such as deserts, forests, grassland, mountain ranges and jungles, which present players with a variety of different features to explore, and unique challenges to face. For example, on a mountain range, players may be faced with uneven, rugged terrain, and with rain and snow, making it difficult to build and mine. Alternatively, in a desert biome, the terrain may be flat but with limited plant life and water, making it difficult to find wood for construction.

Moving from one biome to another within a world provides players with opportunities to find minerals and materials that are unique to specific regions. Players can also encounter structures such as secret temples, complex cave systems and villages, which enable more varied and engaging gameplay.

Mobs

An explanation of Minecraft® would not be complete without a discussion of the many creatures that exist in the Minecraft® universe and can interact with players. These creatures are collectively referred to as 'Mobs' and can be described as falling into four main types – Utility, Neutral, Passive and Hostile.

Utility Mobs are creatures that players can create themselves using items from their inventory, and which attack other Mobs. They can be used to protect a player or a village from Hostile Mobs. Utility Mobs include creatures such as the Iron Golem and the Wither.

Passive Mobs cannot harm players, can sometimes be tamed, and will run away if they are attacked. Passive Mobs include farm animals such as pigs and sheep, tamed animals such as wolves and ocelots, and also Villagers.

Neutral Mobs will only attack if a player provokes them (e.g. if a player attacks the Mob first). Endermen, Spiders (in daylight) and Zombie Pigmen are all considered Neutral.

Finally, there are a number of Hostile Mobs that will attack players that are in close proximity to them. These Mobs are the ones that players in survival mode need to look out for and be prepared to fight, and include Creepers, Skeletons, Zombies and Spiders (at night). There are also several Hostile Mobs that are further described as 'Boss Mobs' due to them having more health than other Mobs which makes them harder to defeat, and also having a larger range in which they can detect players and commence their attack. The 'Boss Mobs' are the Wither, the Elder Guardian and the Ender Dragon.

As this chapter can really only be a brief summary of some of the things you might want to know about Minecraft®, I have included some useful websites at the end of the book that will provide you with tutorials and much broader knowledge if you would like to know more.

Chapter 5

WHY USE MINECRAFT® TO TEACH SOCIAL SKILLS?

The use of technology in education settings has increased significantly in recent years, with devices such as iPads and computers being widely used to assist with communication and learning in schools. Classrooms are invariably equipped with interactive white boards that are used for anything from taking the roll, to solving complex maths equations, to watching a documentary on space, and students are expected to be computer literate to enable them to research topics, create presentations and navigate educational programmes designed to reinforce and extend the skills being taught within the school curriculum.

In this technological age, it makes sense that the use of devices such as computers and iPads would extend into the realm of therapy for children with autism and other developmental difficulties. Computer programs and apps specifically created to teach skills such as regulating emotions, understanding body language and making friends are now widely available for use in schools, therapeutic settings and homes. Further, with the development and popularity of programs such as Minecraft®, teachers and therapists have discovered new and innovative ways to introduce concepts and engage students of all ages and abilities in learning.

So how can Minecraft® be used to teach social skills and what are the benefits of using a computer game as part of a social skills curriculum? As I mentioned in the Introduction, I have found that using Minecraft® has proven to be very effective in supporting social skills development in children with autism for a variety of reasons, not least of which is the lure of using technology and the novelty of playing a computer game while learning. A more detailed discussion of the many benefits of using Minecraft® for teaching social skills will make up the remainder of this chapter.

Technology is often motivating for children with autism

It seems that for many autistic individuals, the lure of a screen is extremely motivating. Many children with autism are drawn to technology, and quickly become skilled in its use, resulting in them seeking to have time on a computer or iPad at any opportunity. As motivation is something that can be difficult to elicit in children with autism, due to their tendency to be focused on their own needs rather than what adults want them to be doing, using a format that is already motivating can assist with increasing engagement in activities and keeping children on task.

Understandably, for many children with autism, talking about social skills is quite difficult, and learning about social skills is certainly not something they would usually choose to spend time doing if they had a choice. Therefore, using technology within a social skills group provides autistic children with a motivating, enjoyable and less threatening way of addressing social skills difficulties and can support engagement and learning.

Minecraft® is an age-appropriate interest that is relevant to typically developing peers

One of the great benefits of Minecraft® is that it is a game that most children of school age have heard of and have played at one time or another. With its wide availability on platforms such as computers, tablets and game consoles, its global merchandising including clothing, figurines and LEGO®, and the popularity of watching professional gamers play on YouTube, it seems rare to find a child who has escaped its influence completely.

Even for those who do not like Minecraft® specifically, many children in their early years of schooling, from around 5 to 13 years of age, are often very interested in computer games, and enjoy sharing their experiences of gameplay and their accomplishments with peers, sometimes even creating role-play games in the playground associated with their favourite gaming characters and adventures.

While many children with autism may struggle to find age-appropriate interests they share with typically developing peers, consequently making social interaction and conversation difficult, the popularity of Minecraft® with school children in particular provides an interest that does not make them 'different' to their same-age peers. Minecraft® can therefore act as common ground in the classroom and playground, giving autistic children a common language in which to communicate and connect with their classmates.

Minecraft® is a common topic of special interest for children with autism

Many children with autism demonstrate intense interest in one or more subjects or activities that may be all consuming and become the focus of almost everything they say and do. Special interests can vary from unusual topics such as vacuum cleaners or air conditioners to interests considered more typical for children such as horses, dinosaurs or trains. While interests can differ greatly between individuals, many autistic children count Minecraft® as one of those special interests, and are extremely motivated to participate in anything Minecraft® related.

This interest and motivation in Minecraft® can be a powerful tool in the effort to teach social skills. It is widely accepted by many educators and allied health professionals that most children demonstrate better engagement and more successful learning when they are interested in what they are doing. With interest comes increased participation, better attention and concentration, and enjoyment of the task, which should increase the likelihood that the information being presented will be retained and hopefully used later on.

Further, an interest in Minecraft® does not just support engagement of tasks that are game-based, but also encourages interest and involvement in learning about social skills concepts when they are presented with a Minecraft® theme and involve Minecraft® characters.

Using Minecraft® therefore not only assists with motivation and engagement, but also supports the successful learning of concepts and strategies presented within the context of the game.

Shared interests allow for more natural interaction between group participants

For children with autism, engaging in conversation and social interaction is often hard work. However, within a group setting where the child knows that all the children in attendance like the same thing, it is much easier and less threatening for them to initiate interactions and have a conversation with a peer.

Not surprisingly, research suggests that when children with autism interact with others around a shared topic of interest, they are more relaxed and better able to communicate effectively. This may be due to them being better able to formulate comments, questions and responses based on their knowledge of the topic and having a more complex vocabulary around their special interest, enabling them to express themselves more confidently. Further, sharing a common interest also provides the opportunity to connect with peers at a more meaningful level and gain enjoyment from social interaction, increasing the possibility of friendships being formed.

Opportunity for participants to share their knowledge and be 'experts'

In a game like Minecraft®, there is an endless supply of new commands, creations and skills that can be mastered while playing, and it is inevitable that within a group of peers, there will be some children who are more skilled at Minecraft® gameplay than others. Rather than this being a problem, this situation provides an opportunity for more skilled players to take on a helping and advisory role within the group, supporting other players when they are unsure how to do something.

Taking on the role of 'expert' within the group can help a child increase their self-confidence and sense of mastery, and develop a feeling of belonging. This can be particularly beneficial for children with autism, as they often struggle with aspects of their learning and behaviour, and as such, may not get many opportunities to demonstrate what they are good at or share their accomplishments with peers.

Being an 'expert' also provides the opportunity for autistic children to practise being patient, understanding and calm when helping someone, and to learn to communicate clearly so others can follow their instructions and successfully complete a task. The child receiving help also has a chance to practise their listening skills, and has to learn to accept the help that is being given and any feedback regarding how well they are completing the task under instruction.

As it is likely that different children will have different skills and knowledge where Minecraft® is concerned, any child within the group has the opportunity to take on the role of 'expert' and share their knowledge at any given time.

Opportunity to practise social skills in 'real' interactions

While playing Minecraft® in the group, children don't just sit silently looking at their screen. Instead, they are engaged in dynamic social interactions with everyone around them including their partners, other group members and the staff. These interactions are usually based on the current gameplay the children are engaged in, and might involve talking to another child about what they are building, asking for help, finding out what others are creating, or planning a joint project.

Facilitators can also encourage children to approach other group members for help or advice, prompt them to compliment another child's work or ask a question about it, and support them to take turns on the computers or when using other materials and equipment. In this way, group members are able to practise using a variety of social skills, including the specific skills we discuss in the session and other incidental social skills, as they are naturally required within the group setting.

Learning to manage conflict

It is the nature of computer games being played by multiple children at once that at some point a conflict will arise due to the actions of one or more of the players. For example, a dispute may occur over the ownership of materials that have been found or the location in which a player wants to build, or there might be conflict following one player destroying the house of another in the game. These situations provide the perfect opportunity to support the players involved to problem solve and find a solution, and to regulate their emotions and behaviour effectively.

In some cases, group members may be able to manage the conflict themselves, talking through the problem and how it might be fixed, especially when something has occurred by accident during play. At other times, an adult may be needed to support the children involved to remain calm, consider the other person's point of view, and consider possible solutions.

As you can see, there are many benefits to using Minecraft® to support social skills development in children with autism. In the next chapter, I will take you through what you will need to set up your own Minecraft® group at your school, practice or organization.

PART 2

PUTTING IT ALL TOGETHER

Chapter 6

GETTING SET UP

Given the popularity of Minecraft® and its worldwide use, there are many websites and tutorials available online that provide great information about setting up computers and Minecraft® accounts, downloading Minecraft® and getting started with gameplay. That being said, there are a few things that we have learned along the way that will hopefully help you get set up and running your group stress free, and we would like to share these tips with you.

This chapter will briefly summarize some of the technical requirements you need to be aware of and refer you to more detailed information where required, as well as providing you with the tips and tricks that have helped us get set up for groups with minimal fuss.

Platforms/devices

Before you can start planning your Minecraft® group, you will need to decide what platform you are going to use. It is important to keep in mind that you will need to have one device for every two children attending the group, and all devices will need to use the same version of Minecraft®. Having identical devices is recommended where possible to ensure consistency across the group with regard to controls and set-up.

For our groups, we use five Mac desktop computers which will accommodate ten group participants. Alternatively, you could use Windows PCs or laptops. While iPads or

tablets could also be used for the group programme, we have found that using computers provides the best possible opportunity for interaction between group members due to the table set-up which allows for children to sit side by side and larger screens to support a shared experience.

Technical requirements

To ensure your devices are able to support the most recent version of Minecraft®, it is best to visit the Mojang support page (help.mojang.com) for the necessary specifications. There are also demo versions that can be downloaded to check whether your device is powerful enough to run the program.

You will need a stable and strong internet connection that is capable of carrying the load of several devices being connected to Minecraft® at once, and may choose to connect your computers by Wi-Fi or by a wired network connection. Where possible, it is best to have a dedicated internet connection for the program, as other users of the same network (e.g. staff members, other students) may experience slower internet access as a result of the group.

Creating a Minecraft® account

To get started on your Minecraft® journey, you will need to first create a Mojang account and pay for and download Minecraft® on each computer. This is easily done from the official Minecraft® website: Minecraft.net.

As there will be multiple players using Realms at any one time (one player on each computer), each computer will need a Mojang account assigned to it. These can be created for free using a unique email address for each player.

When we first set up our computers for groups, we had to create five new email addresses in order to set up the player accounts. To do this, we set up individual email addresses on Gmail however, addresses can be created on any system you have access to (e.g. business email addresses, school accounts, etc.).

Minecraft® Realms

Next, you will need to purchase Minecraft® Realms on one computer using one of your Minecraft® accounts. This account will act as the admin for the Realms server and will be used to control the various options associated with the Minecraft® world that is used.

Minecraft® Realms is a version of Minecraft® that allows friends to play together on a secure server where only invited players can join. We chose this platform for our groups as it allows us to control both which players are in the world and the characteristics of the world itself, without the possibility of external players getting access. Minecraft® Realms is a subscription service in which users can sign up for just one month or for longer periods of time. One Minecraft® Realms subscription for PC or Mac allows for the user who purchased the subscription and ten other players to access the Realm. On Minecraft® for mobile, console and Windows, a subscription for up to 3 or up to 11 players is available.

As we use Mac computers in our groups, we use the Java edition of Minecraft® Realms, which is suitable for use on Macs and PCs. More detailed information about Realms and how to purchase a subscription is available at Minecraft.net.

Creating/selecting worlds

Once your set-up of Realms is complete, you will usually have three worlds available to you that you can tailor to your needs.

Each world can be edited by selecting from several options which allow you to choose from a random world with qualities such as being 'superflat' or containing structures, world templates that include places such as jungle villages or castles, and adventure templates which contain more complex settings. You can prepare each of the three worlds with the setting of your choice, but only one world can be used to play in at a time.

When we run groups, we often pre-prepare worlds to suit the activities that are planned for a session. For example, we may use a 'superflat' world when group participants are going to be creating pictures or pixel art, or a mountainous world when the activity for the session is to build a rollercoaster.

It is important to note that if you require multiple worlds to be available to use in one session (e.g. one world to complete activities in and one world to have free-play or destroy things), then you may need to purchase another Realm using another player's Mojang account.

World options

Within each world, there are options available to change settings regarding the mode of play and the features that the world will include.

For our groups, we always play in creative mode so that no one's character can be injured or killed during play. We also always turn off 'PvP', which stands for player versus player, so that players cannot attack each other. Other settings, such as Mobs or animals being spawned in the world, can be turned off or on as needed.

Inviting players

The final step in the set-up process is to invite other players to join your Realm. This involves the player who purchased the Realm and is acting as 'admin' selecting the option to invite players. The names of each of the other players that have been created for the group then need to be entered into the admin computer and an invitation will be sent to them. Once the other player logins are used to open Minecraft® on the other group computers and Realms is selected, an invitation will appear as a message at the top of the screen. Each invitation will need to be accepted to allow each player to access the world that has been created for the group.

Setting up the group room

When you are ready to run your group, it is important to consider not just the computers, but also how you will set up your room. Ideally, you will have a large enough space to include five computers on tables, with two chairs at each table, an area for group participants to sit on the floor during group discussions, and a space for movement breaks and alternative activities (see Chapter 7 for more information).

The computers should be arranged to allow opportunity for interaction not just between each member of a pair, but between pairs as well. This provides more possibilities for positive social interaction between group members. For example, arrangement of tables in the shape of a 'C' allows for interactions between all participants (Figure 6.1).

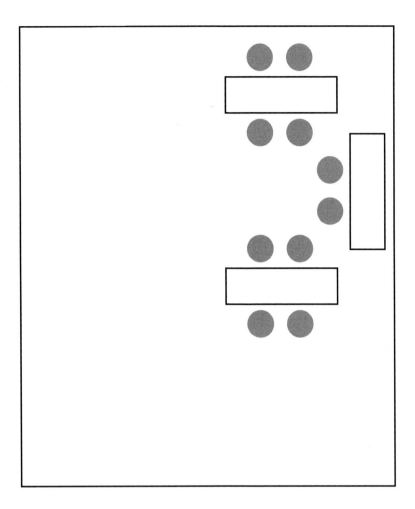

Figure 6.1 Sample room set-up

If you have limited space to run the group, or fewer than ten participants, you may need to arrange things differently. As long as the space is comfortable and workable for you, then it will be fine. Where possible, when the group room is small, it would be a good idea to prepare an alternative room or area to use as a 'breakout' space for any children who need a break from the group for any reason.

Chapter 7

RUNNING THE PROGRAMME

Now that you know why it is important to teach social skills to children with autism, the benefits of using a Minecraft®-themed programme, and what resources you will need to effectively run the programme, it is time to talk about the way the programme is structured and what a typical session looks like.

Participants

The programme is designed primarily for children aged 5–12 years who have a diagnosis of autism spectrum disorder or other social difficulties and are attending mainstream school. Groups ideally consist of eight to ten children of similar age. At our practice, we usually arrange the groups according to year levels, with children in Prep/Foundation–Grade 3, or Grade 4–6, attending together; however, it would be appropriate for children all to be in the same year level or from a wider range of grades depending on the setting and the children wanting to attend.

Staffing

For a group of eight to ten children, I recommend a minimum of two staff members, as this allows for one to facilitate the group while the other assists with behaviour management and providing support where needed. In a setting such as a school or with a smaller group size, one staff member may be sufficient; however, this would also depend on the needs of the children participating. We have been fortunate to have had access to psychology students from a local university who volunteer to assist with our groups, which has enabled us to have a higher adult-to-child ratio, and provided participants with additional support during the group programmes. Offering volunteer opportunities to university students in your local area who are completing qualifications in allied health or education can be a great way of having additional staff assist with running the groups.

Programme structure

The full programme consists of thirty 90-minute sessions. The sessions have been grouped into blocks of five that include the introduction of four social skills topics and a review session within each block. This structure ensures that the information presented in each session is reviewed at least once following its introduction, and is viewed in the context of other social skills rather than being discussed in isolation.

While it is useful to run sessions in the blocks suggested, the programme materials are also able to be used independently, allowing for facilitators to handpick topics that will specifically target the skill deficits of their group members where required.

Session format

Each session follows a simple format that allows for the introduction of social skills topics and direct teaching by the facilitator, group discussion with participants, structured Minecraft® activities on the computers, and unstructured time that provides the opportunity for practising social interaction with peers. Depending on the children attending the group, it may also be necessary to schedule in movement breaks and alternative activities to cater to varied sensory needs and interests. Table 7.1 provides an example of the basic session structure and time allocated to each activity.

Table 7.1 Example of session structure

Time	Activity
5 min	Review group rules and home challenge from previous session
10 min	Introduce social skills topic and discuss with the group
10 min	Explain today's computer activity and discuss with the group
10 min	Player 1 starts activity on the computer
10 min	Player 2 starts activity on the computer
5 min	Movement break
5 min	Peer discussion of activities

Time	Activity
5 min	Discuss social skills topic further (if appropriate) and explain plan for the next computer activity
10 min	Player 1 completes activity or has free play
10 min	Player 2 completes activity or has free play
10 min	Explain home challenge and give rewards
	Finish

The allocation of specific time frames to individual activities is helpful to keep the session flowing and ensure that essential information is covered; however, flexibility within the session is also important. For example, if participants are working well together completing an activity on the computers, it may be more beneficial to their development of social skills to allow them to continue for a few minutes past the allocated time and have an extended positive interaction than interrupting them to follow the schedule exactly. Regardless of the specific topic of a session, any spontaneous positive social interaction between participants is something to be encouraged, as using social skills appropriately and naturally is the ultimate goal of any social skills group.

Session activities

Introducing and discussing the social skills topic

To introduce the social skills topic for each session, I find it works best to let the participants know what we are going to be talking about and ask them what they already know about the topic (e.g. 'Today we are going to talk about having a conversation. Who knows what a conversation is?'). This really helps the participants get involved from the beginning, and helps direct further discussion of the topic. If your participants don't have anything to say, have a few suggestions of your own to assist them with ideas.

Using visuals to highlight the main points or concepts related to the topic is also useful, as you can break the skill down and discuss each point with an associated visual cue to enhance understanding and assist with keeping their attention. The main points for each topic are included in the handout for each session, and this can be used as the visual for the discussion. If you feel that using larger visuals will be most effective, you can print out the session handout on A3 paper to have more of an impact.

Once you have presented the main points that you want participants to understand, a discussion of why the skill is important, and when and where they might use the skill, helps to relate what they have learned to applications in real life. Ask for examples of when they have used the skills before, and have your own examples and scenarios ready just in case.

Explaining the computer activity and planning

The computer activities that are planned for each session are designed to provide an initial focus and structure for the participants when working on the computers with their partners. When introducing the activity for the day, talk to the participants about details such as what their creation might look like, what features might be essential to include, and what materials they might like to use. For some activities, participants will also need time to work with a partner to discuss and plan what they will do before they go to the computers to start their work.

Computer work

When it is time for participants to work on the computers, they need to form pairs. You can do this by allowing participants to choose their own partners or by allocating children to specific pairs. As you may not have met the participants before the first session, it is important to observe the dynamics between the participants and take note of any combinations of children that might be worthwhile encouraging or avoiding in future sessions to facilitate positive interactions.

When participants initially move to the computers, they need to establish who will have a turn first. This can be done through negotiation between participants or by using a method such as 'Rock, Paper, Scissors' if an agreement can't be reached.

Once they commence computer work, the focus is initially on completing the set task for the session. The first participant is given a ten-minute block on the computers, and then needs to swap with their partner so he or she can have a ten-minute turn. Following some further discussion in the middle of the session, each child will have the opportunity for another ten-minute block on the computer.

Some children will need assistance and encouragement to stay on task and complete the activity, or need support to understand what to do and how to do it. This is a great opportunity to encourage participants with more advanced Minecraft® skills to assist their partners or other group members with the task and share their knowledge.

It can also be difficult for participants to wait for their turn while their partner is on the computer. I usually encourage partners to stay together and support each other during the first block of computer time, and then give them the option of doing some other activities while they wait for their turn during the second computer block. Some ideas for appropriate alternative activities are included later in this chapter.

When the set task has been completed, participants should be given an opportunity to engage in free play. This is best done by providing participants with an alternative world to log in to in which they can do whatever they want, without impacting on the creations of other group members. In my experience, free play time is often where you see participants increasingly engage in spontaneous social interactions with their peers. As they get to know each other through the sessions and build their confidence, participants often spontaneously create a challenge or activity to engage in (e.g. building a portal and fighting the Ender Dragon) and try to recruit others to assist them, providing the opportunity for them to work together and share enjoyment in achieving a goal.

Movement breaks

As mentioned earlier, movement breaks may be necessary for some children to assist them to regulate their arousal levels and to receive sensory input, stretch their legs and refocus. It is important to be aware of which activities are settling or calming for participants and which activities may heighten arousal. Typically, activities that involve firm pressure on joints (e.g. climbing, pushing, jumping and crashing) are regulating and settling for most children, but there are always exceptions.

When I run my groups, we set up an obstacle course that includes crawling on a pile of cushions, rolling along a gym mat, bouncing on a mini trampoline and running and jumping into a crash mat. Alternatively, you could play a group game, do gross motor activities such as crab walks or pushing on a wall, or even do some yoga. Obviously, you will need to consider the amount of space you have and what equipment you have access to before deciding on movement break activities for your group. If you are not sure or need more ideas, consulting an occupational therapist can be useful.

Peer discussion of activities

Setting some time for participants to speak to each other about what they have created on the computers provides them with an opportunity to practise conversation skills such as asking and answering questions, showing interest and listening while talking about something that they really like. Some participants may need an adult to facilitate this interaction by suggesting questions they can ask, encouraging participants to share their thoughts, and assisting them to keep the momentum of a reciprocal interaction going.

Home challenge

Providing an activity for participants to take home and complete creates an opportunity for participants to think about and practise a specific skill outside the group environment. It also provides parents with an opportunity to assist their child with learning around the specific topic. The home challenge for each topic is included in the handout participants take home after each session.

You will need to take a few minutes at the end of each session to show participants the handout and explain what is required to complete it. Then you can discuss the challenge at the beginning of the next session and ask participants to share their experience of completing the task or their responses to the questions that were given. Sometimes participants will be reluctant to speak in front of the group. In these situations you can offer to share their response for them (if it is written down) or encourage them to listen to their peers while they share their ideas. Do not try to make them speak to the group if they don't want to.

It is also important to note that there will always be participants who do not do their home challenge for various reasons. If this occurs, include the participant in the discussions as usual and assist them to reflect on how they might have responded if they had completed the task.

Alternative activities

Having additional activities available for participants is useful, particularly for children who have difficulty waiting for their turn on the computers or lose interest in working on the computers throughout the session. These activities provide an alternative opportunity for social interaction in a less structured way, and also support the practice of other skills such as winning and losing, sharing and taking turns. Activities could include Minecraft® colouring pages and word searches, Minecraft® papercraft, board games, card games or craft (e.g. bead art, cutting and pasting, etc.). Many of the craft and colouring resources are freely available online to download and use. I have included some useful resource websites later in the book for your reference. You will also find a Minecraft®-themed Snakes and Ladders game in the Appendix that can be printed for use during sessions.

Behaviour management strategies

Group rules

Setting clear expectations and boundaries right at the beginning of any group is very important, so one of the first activities that needs to be completed in the first session is establishing group rules. Once agreed upon, these rules can be referred to and reviewed in subsequent sessions to help maintain a positive group environment.

When discussing group rules with participants, it is important to encourage ideas from group members regarding what rules might be needed to ensure everyone feels happy and safe attending the sessions, and why following the rules is so important. As with other discussions, have your own ideas ready in case the participants are having difficulty thinking of appropriate suggestions, or they leave something out that you think is important.

Some common rules that are worthwhile considering are:

- 'Hands, feet and objects to yourself': This is a rule that most children have come across at school in some form to reinforce not touching or hitting others.

- 'If you make it, you can break it': This is a rule I always include in these groups, as it refers to damaging other people's creations in Minecraft®. Basically, it is all right for a child to destroy something they have made themselves, but not all right to damage anyone else's structures.

- 'One person talking at a time': It can be helpful to highlight the expectation that participants will take turns to talk and listen when others are talking, rather than everyone talking over the top of each other.

- 'Use nice/kind words and no swearing': Although the concept of 'nice' or 'kind' can sometimes be difficult to grasp, most children are aware of words that are appropriate to say and words that are not, and reminding participants that this is expected behaviour is useful.

Visual schedule

Children with autism often experience anxiety when in new situations and with new people, so attending a group for the first time is likely to be quite stressful. Further, it can take a while for children to settle in and feel comfortable – perhaps several sessions – so it is important to provide a predictable and safe environment for them to operate in that reduces their feelings of discomfort.

The use of a visual schedule is a great way to reduce the anxiety of participants by making each session more predictable. A visual schedule most often involves a series of pictures representing each activity or part of a programme, which are displayed vertically on a board or wall in order of their occurrence. This allows a child to look at the schedule and see what activities are going to occur, in what order, and when the session will be finished. For example, a visual schedule for a typical Minecraft® group might include: Saying hello; Group discussion; Today's activity; Computer work; Movement break; Group discussion; Computer work; Home challenge and reward. Examples of visual schedule cards are included in Chapter 8.

Sensory tools

Many children with autism and other developmental difficulties have problems with sensory processing and integration. This can make it very difficult for them to sit still and attend during discussions and participate fully in activities without some sensory accommodations being made. Accommodations may include allowing a child who requires movement when concentrating to sit at the back of the group and move around during discussions, or allowing the use of cushions, fidget toys or weighted objects to assist children to stay focused.

Reward system

In my experience working with children with autism, I have found that it is often helpful to use a reward system to encourage positive behaviour in a variety of settings. Introducing a reward system into a group programme can help to motivate participants to follow rules and make good choices about their behaviour in an effort to earn a reward at the end of the session. When considering the use of a reward system, it is important to consider what behaviour you want to encourage, whether the reward will be given immediately or earned after a certain number of behaviours have been observed, and how the positive behaviour will be recorded (e.g. stickers, ticks, tokens).

It is also important not to take away rewards that have been earned due to inappropriate behaviour. We want to focus on the good choices a child is making, and this means that these choices need to be acknowledged and rewarded without the fear of them being taken away. In the majority of situations, when a child makes an inappropriate choice, it will be enough to remind the child of the rules, and tell them what is expected. Then the child should be allowed to continue what they are doing to demonstrate that they can do it appropriately. If a child does act in an inappropriate way and a consequence is required, this needs to be a more natural response to the behaviour. For example, for a child who continues to destroy a group member's Minecraft® house after being reminded of the rules several times, they might need to take a break from the computer for a few minutes and lose part of their turn, before being allowed to continue with the activity.

If you choose to use a reward system in your group, an explanation of exactly what participants need to do to earn rewards, and what the reward will be, should occur at the start of the first session.

When we run our groups, we use a reward system composed of 'Minecraft® dollars' and a prize box. Participants are instructed that they can earn 'Minecraft® dollars' by engaging in positive behaviours including following the group rules, using the specific social skill introduced for the session, participating in discussions and helping other group members. For every five Minecraft® dollars earned, participants can choose a prize from the prize box at the end of the session. Minecraft® dollars are given out regularly throughout the session by facilitators, to keep participants motivated and thinking about their behaviour. The prizes we use are small but motivating such as mini Minecraft® figures, lollipops, bouncy balls, stretchy lizards and bubbles. Wherever possible, we try to ensure that all participants earn enough dollars for at least one prize by the end of each session. A template for Minecraft® dollars is included in the Resources section at the end of the book.

Chapter 8

SESSION PLANS AND HANDOUTS

This chapter includes detailed session plans for facilitators, and handouts to provide to participants and their families, as well as additional information to assist with preparing for and running each social skills session.

SESSION 1: COMMUNICATION

World set-up

The world for this session should be one in which the students can explore and find treasure. When using Minecraft® Realms, I usually choose a premade world such as 'Raider's Refuge' which has a large pirate's hideout to use as a base, water surrounding it to sail in, and lots of different areas to explore.

You will need to spend some time before the session placing chests around the world and filling them with treasure. There will also be chests already located in different places throughout the buildings that you can utilize too. You can place items from your inventory including gold and iron ingots, diamonds, emeralds, swords, pickaxes and armour, as well as novelty items such as cakes or golden apples. Vary the amount of each item in the world so some are more common than others – this makes for some interesting conversation when students are discussing what they have found.

Computer activity

The first computer activity involves students moving around the world searching for and collecting treasure from the chests that have been placed there.

The second computer activity is to craft a boat and then explore the water around the island. Students will need to use a crafting table and follow the recipe on the handout to create the boat.

KEY POINTS FOR DISCUSSION

- What is communication? How do we communicate our thoughts and feelings to others? (e.g. How would you know if I was feeling angry?) – words, actions, facial expression, body language, tone of voice

- What does good communication involve? – refer to handout

- Do you ever find it difficult to communicate? When?

- What happens when someone does not communicate clearly?

- Are there other ways you can get your message across to someone without talking?

SKILLS TO HIGHLIGHT DURING THE SESSION

- Sharing information

- Taking turns to talk

- Giving instructions

COMMUNICATION – SESSION PLAN

Time	Activity
5 min	Welcome and Introductions
10 min	Group Rules and Minecraft® money
10 min	What is Communication? Talk as a group about how we communicate with others
5 min	Discuss today's activity – exploring Pirate Island. Talk with the group about how to move around the island, what to look for, etc.
10 min	Player 1 explores Pirate Island and collects materials
10 min	Player 2 explores Pirate Island and collects materials
5 min	Movement Break
10 min	Check inventory. Talk to others about what they have collected. Collect supplies to make a boat. Review crafting recipe.
10 min	Player 1 crafts a boat and explores the water
10 min	Player 2 crafts a boat and explores the water
5 min	Explain Home Challenge and Give Rewards
	Finish

COMMUNICATION

Today we practised our Communication Skills during the following activities:

o With the group, we discussed the different ways we communicate and what good communication looks like.

o With partners, we searched a Pirate Island for chests containing treasure.

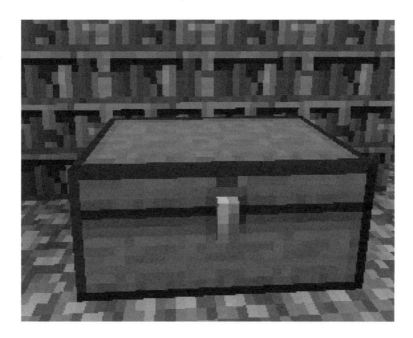

o With the group, we discussed what kinds of treasure were found on the island.
  • What did they find?
  • Where did they find it?

o With partners, we helped each other build boats and explored the water around the island.

COMMUNICATION

What are good Communication Skills?

Start or end the conversation.
Say 'Hello' or 'Goodbye'.

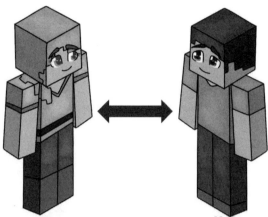

Look at the person you are talking to.
Turn your body towards the person.

Ask and answer questions.
Listen to what is being said.

Take turns to talk.
Talk about the same thing.

COMMUNICATION

Home Challenge

Using your Communication Skills:

○ Teach a family member (e.g. Mum, Dad, grandparent, brother or sister) how to craft a boat in Minecraft®.

○ Then help them take the boat out on some water for a ride.

NB: You will need five wood planks to make a boat (and a wooden shovel if using Minecraft® on the iPad).

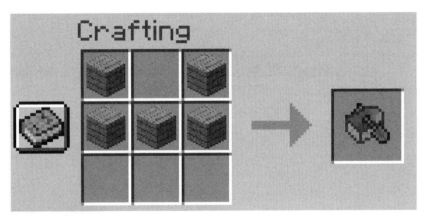

SESSION 2: CREATIVITY

World set-up

For this session, the world should be flat or at least have some flat areas so students can build. In Minecraft® Realms, you can generate a new world that is flat with no structures if required.

Computer activity

The computer activity for this session involves building a house and accompanying garden. Students can use all of their allocated computer time to complete a detailed design, or can make something more simple and then engage in free play (preferably in an alternative world so they do not interfere with the work of others).

KEY POINTS FOR DISCUSSION

· What does being creative mean? What are some ways that you are creative?

· What does being creative involve? – refer to handout

· How can being creative help us at school, at home and with our friends?
  e.g. think of ideas for games to play, be flexible when a friend wants to play something different, find a way to solve a problem at home, etc.

SKILLS TO HIGHLIGHT DURING THE SESSION

· Flexible thinking

· Imaginative ideas

· Problem solving

CREATIVITY – SESSION PLAN

Time	Activity
5 min	Welcome
5 min	Review Group Rules and Home Challenge
10 min	What is Creativity? Talk as a group about what it means to be creative – flexibility, problem solving, imaginative.
10 min	Discuss today's activity – building a house. Talk with the group about what features a house needs, what it can be made of, etc.
10 min	Player 1 designs and builds a house
10 min	Player 2 designs and builds a house
5 min	Movement Break
10 min	Discuss what features they have included in their houses so far. What else would be good to add?
10 min	Player 1 continues to build house and garden
10 min	Player 2 continues to build house and garden
5 min	Explain Home Challenge and Give Rewards
	Finish

CREATIVITY

Today we practised being Creative during the following activities:

○ With the group, we discussed what being creative involves and how creativity helps us to think of ideas and find solutions to problems.

○ Working with partners, we built houses in Minecraft®. We had to consider:
  • Where to build
  • Materials to use
  • Design
  • Features (number and type of rooms, furniture, etc.).

CREATIVITY

How can we be Creative?

Be flexible

Use your imagination

Think about your choices

CREATIVITY

Home Challenge

Using your Creativity:

o Draw yourself as a Minecraft® character:
- What would you wear? (e.g. clothes, armour, etc.)
- What weapon would you have?

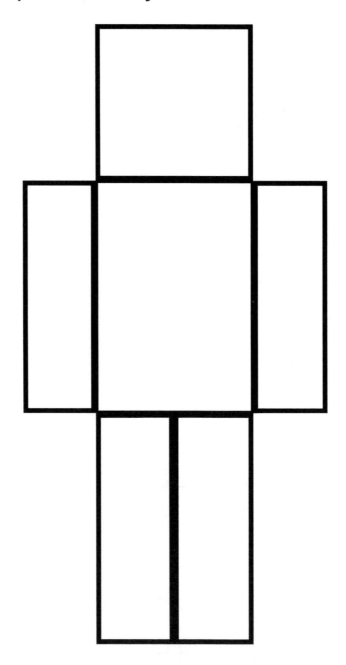

SESSION 3: FRIENDSHIP

World set-up

In this session, the world needs to be flat or feature large open spaces, to enable students to create pixel art.

Computer activity

Students will create pixel art for their computer activity, which involves using coloured blocks to create a 2-D image. Students may choose to create their own design, or copy one. It is recommended that an assortment of designs be downloaded and printed before the session and be made available to the students for ideas. Pixel art patterns are available from many online sources, including Google Images, using the search term 'pixel art' and the name of an object or character (e.g. 'pokemon pixel art').

KEY POINTS FOR DISCUSSION

- What is a friend? How do you know that someone is your friend?

- What makes a good friend? – refer to handout

- What is friendly behaviour?

- What do you like to do with your friends?

- What can you say to let your friend know you like something they are doing? Give a compliment (see home challenge for details)

- How does it feel to get a compliment from someone?

SKILLS TO HIGHLIGHT DURING THE SESSION

- Sharing and taking turns

- Helping others

- Working together

- Giving compliments

FRIENDSHIP – SESSION PLAN

Time	Activity
5 min	Welcome
5 min	Review Home Challenge
10 min	What is Friendship? Talk as a group about what makes a good friend – similar interests, caring, helpful, encouraging, having fun together, talking to each other.
10 min	Discuss today's activity – creating pixel art. Talk with the group about how to create pixel art on Minecraft® – following a pattern, choosing correct coloured blocks, etc. Each pair should choose two designs to make.
10 min	Player 1 creates pixel art
10 min	Player 2 creates pixel art
5 min	Movement Break
10 min	Discuss what they have created. Was it easy/hard? How did they help each other with their art?
10 min	Player 1 pixel art and Free Play
10 min	Player 2 pixel art and Free Play
5 min	Explain Home Challenge and Give Rewards
	Finish

FRIENDSHIP

Today we practised the skills required to be a good Friend during the following activities:

o With the group, we discussed what makes a good friend and how we can encourage and compliment our friends.

o Working with partners, we made pixel art in Minecraft®. We had to:
- Decide on a picture to make together
- Choose materials to use
- Follow the pattern
- Encourage our partners and compliment their efforts.

FRIENDSHIP

What makes a good Friend?

Like some of the same things.

Care about each other.

Talk and listen to each other.

Have fun together.

Help each other.

FRIENDSHIP

Home Challenge

Giving compliments:

Before the next session, practise giving at least three compliments to members of your family or friends.

Remember, when you are giving a compliment:
- ! Be positive
- ! Be honest
- ! Be as specific as you can
- ! Think about what you like about the person or what they do.

For example:

'Thanks Mum, dinner was really yummy.'

'I like the way you drew that rainbow.'

'Your Minecraft® t-shirt is cool!'

SESSION 4: COOPERATION

World set-up

The world for this session is ideally one with some mountains or hilly landscape to support the construction of rollercoasters. Mountains give students an elevated starting point from which they can build their rollercoasters. Most randomly generated worlds should include some of these features.

Computer activity

Building a rollercoaster is the main activity for this session. Before going on the computers, encourage pairs to start to talk about ideas and design their rollercoasters on paper. Once they have an idea of what they want to build, students can go on the computers.

While it is hoped that each pair will make one rollercoaster between them, it is all right for each student to make their own when it is their turn on the computer.

To construct a rollercoaster, students will need standard rails, powered rails and a minecart from their inventory. Standard rails can be used for any downward parts of the rollercoaster and corners, and powered rails should be used when uphill movement is required.

KEY POINTS FOR DISCUSSION

- What is cooperation? – working together to achieve something

- Why is it important to cooperate? – makes things easier, faster, helpful, etc.

- How do we cooperate with others? – refer to handout

- When have you cooperated with others at home or school?

- What is compromising? – refer to handout

SKILLS TO HIGHLIGHT DURING THE SESSION

- Listening to others

- Compromising

- Working together

- Using nice words

COOPERATION – SESSION PLAN

Time	Activity
5 min	Welcome
5 min	Review Home Challenge
10 min	What is Cooperation? Talk as a group about what it means to cooperate – work together to achieve something. Ask for examples of when the group have cooperated.
10 min	Discuss today's activity – making a rollercoaster. Talk with the group about cooperating to build with their partners. Discuss materials, placement, types of rails, etc.
5 min	Design rollercoasters in pairs
10 min	Player 1 builds rollercoaster
10 min	Player 2 builds rollercoaster
5 min	Movement Break
5 min	Discuss what features they have included in their rollercoasters
10 min	Player 1 continues to build rollercoaster or Free Play
10 min	Player 2 continues to build rollercoaster or Free Play
5 min	Explain Home Challenge and Give Rewards
	Finish

COOPERATION

Today we practised the skills required to Cooperate with others during the following activities:

○ With the group, we discussed what being cooperative looks like and why cooperating is important.

○ Working with partners, we made rollercoasters in Minecraft®. We had to:
- Design a rollercoaster
- Choose materials
- Listen to each other's ideas
- Compromise
- Divide up tasks
- Encourage our partner and compliment their effort.

COOPERATION

What is good Cooperation?

Help each other

Listen to each other's ideas

Show respect for each other

Use nice words

Share the work

Compromise

COOPERATION

What is compromising?

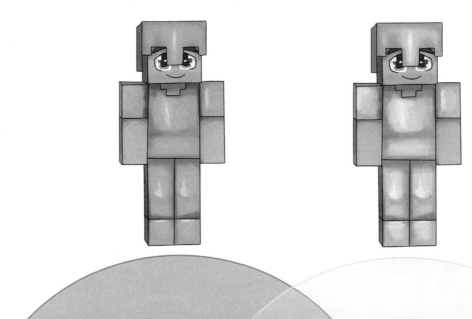

I WANT...   COMPROMISE   YOU WANT...

COOPERATION

Home Challenge

When do you Cooperate?

o Find an opportunity to cooperate with your parents or siblings before our next session.

o Discuss the following questions with your family:
- Did cooperating make the job easier or harder?
- How did your parents or siblings feel when you cooperated?
- How did you feel?

For example:

o Help your brother or sister pack up some toys.
o Help Mum or Dad prepare dinner.
o Build a LEGO® spaceship with your dad.
o Help clear the dishes off the table after dinner.

SESSION 5: PUTTING IT ALL TOGETHER – SUMMARY SESSION

World set-up

The world for this session is ideally flat to allow room for the students to construct farmhouses and animal enclosures.

Computer activity

In this session, students will work together to create a farm. Before going on the computers, discuss the types of features a farm may need and appropriate animals or crops to grow, and if possible, allocate a specific part of the farm to each pair.

Everything students may need for building a farm, including fences and 'eggs' to spawn farm animals, can be found in the student's inventory.

KEY POINTS FOR DISCUSSION

· What is good communication?

· How can being creative help us at school and at home?

· What is a friend?

· How do we cooperate with others?

· What does compromising mean?

SKILLS TO HIGHLIGHT DURING THE SESSION

· Communication (e.g. talking together, staying on topic, looking at the person, etc.)

· Creativity (e.g. flexible thinking, imagination, problem solving, etc.)

· Friendly behaviour (e.g. helping each other, using nice words, giving compliments, etc.)

· Cooperation (e.g. working together, compromising, using nice words, etc.)

PUTTING IT ALL TOGETHER – SESSION PLAN

Time	Activity
5 min	Welcome
5 min	Review Home Challenge
10 min	What have we learned about this week? ○ Communication ○ Creativity ○ Friendship ○ Cooperation Talk as a group about what we have learned and how we can use this information at school and at home.
10 min	Discuss today's activity – making a farm. Decide as a group what animals to put on the farm, who will build enclosures, who will spawn the animals, etc.
10 min	Player 1 builds farm
10 min	Player 2 builds farm
5 min	Movement Break
10 min	Discuss what they have created. Was it easy/hard? How did they work together/communicate/create/support?
10 min	Player 1 builds farm or Free Play
10 min	Player 2 builds farm or Free Play
5 min	Give Certificates and Rewards
	Finish

PUTTING IT ALL TOGETHER

Today we reviewed and practised the skills we have learned over the last few sessions during the following activities:

o With the group, we discussed what we have learned and how we can use these skills at home and at school.

o Working as a team, we made a farm in Minecraft®. We had to:
- COMMUNICATE clearly
- Be CREATIVE and flexible
- Encourage and support each of our FRIENDS
- COOPERATE with each other.

SESSION 6: POINT OF VIEW

World set-up

In this session, the world needs to be flat or feature large open spaces, to enable students to create pixel art.

Computer activity

Students will create pixel art for their computer activity, which involves using coloured blocks to create a 2-D image. Students may choose to create their own design, or copy one. Pixel art patterns are available from many online sources including Google Images, using the search term 'pixel art' and the name of an object or character (e.g. 'pokemon pixel art').

KEY POINTS FOR DISCUSSION

- Why do Steve and Alex see the same Creeper in different ways? – refer to handout

- How can people sometimes see different pictures in optical illusions? – refer to handout (NB: Having additional optical illusions to look at can be useful)

- What impact does having a different point of view have in social situations?

- Why is it important to respect another person's point of view?

- What is the difference between a fact and an opinion? – refer to handout

- Can we still be friends with someone who has a different opinion than we do?

SKILLS TO HIGHLIGHT DURING THE SESSION

- Respecting other opinions and points of view

- Using nice words

UNDERSTANDING POINT OF VIEW SESSION PLAN

Time	Activity
5 min	Welcome and Introductions
10 min	Group Rules and Minecraft® money
10 min	Understanding Point of View Talk as a group about how others might see and interpret things differently to us. Discuss why it is important to consider another's point of view.
5 min	Discuss today's activity – creating pixel art. Talk with the group about how to create pixel art on Minecraft® – following a pattern, choosing correct coloured blocks, etc.
10 min	Player 1 makes pixel art
10 min	Player 2 makes pixel art
5 min	Movement Break
10 min	Opinion vs Fact. Talk about the difference between fact and opinion and why it is all right for others to have a different opinion. Discuss examples of opinions and facts.
10 min	Player 1 makes armour and a weapon that they think is the best
10 min	Player 2 makes armour and a weapon that they think is the best
5 min	Explain Home Challenge and Give Rewards
	Finish

UNDERSTANDING POINT OF VIEW

Today we learned about different Points of View during the following activities:

o With the group, we discussed the difference between a fact and an opinion.
  - Is it OK to have a different opinion to someone else?
  - How can we accept another's opinion when we don't agree?

o With partners, we created pixel art. We discussed how pixel art looks up close and far away. Does it look different from another point of view?

o On the computer, we each created our favourite armour and weapon for a character. We discussed how our choice might be different to our partner's.

UNDERSTANDING POINT OF VIEW

How big is the Creeper from Steve's Point of View?

What do you see in the picture below?

UNDERSTANDING POINT OF VIEW

Opinion vs Fact

FACT – A thing that is known or can be proven to be true.

For example:

Creepers are creatures in Minecraft®.

OPINION – A belief, thought or feeling about something.

For example:

Minecraft® is fun!

UNDERSTANDING POINT OF VIEW

Home Challenge

Fact vs Opinion:

For each of the sentences below, underline the <u>facts</u> in blue and the <u>opinions</u> in red.

A skateboard has four wheels.

Baby ducks are called ducklings.

Basketball is a fun sport.

The Earth is a planet.

It's easy to win UNO®.

Minecraft® is better than Terraria®.

Swimming is a water sport.

Cats make better pets than dogs.

Jam tastes good on toast.

SESSION 7: BY ACCIDENT OR ON PURPOSE

World set-up

The world for this session is ideally one with some mountains or hilly landscape to support the construction of waterslides. Mountains give students an elevated starting point from which they can build their waterslides.

Computer activity

Building a waterslide is the main activity for this session. Before going on the computers, encourage pairs to start to talk about ideas and design their waterslides on paper. Once they have an idea of what they want to build, students can go on the computers.

While it is hoped that each pair will make one waterslide between them, it is all right for each student to make their own when it is their turn on the computer.

A waterslide can be made by cutting into the side of a mountain to create a crevasse in which water can travel down, or by constructing a slide with edges to hold the water. To add water, students can use a water bucket from their inventory and place it at the top of their slide to start the water flowing.

KEY POINTS FOR DISCUSSION

- What do we mean when we say someone did something by accident or on purpose?

- How can we tell that someone has done something by accident? – refer to handout

- How can we tell that someone has done something on purpose? – refer to handout

- Do we still need to apologize when we do something by accident?

SKILLS TO HIGHLIGHT DURING THE SESSION

- Cooperation

- Using nice words

- Apologizing if someone breaks something in Minecraft® by accident

- Flexible thinking

- Staying calm

- Encouraging others

BY ACCIDENT OR ON PURPOSE – SESSION PLAN

Time	Activity
5 min	Welcome
5 min	Review Group Rules and Home Challenge
10 min	What do we mean when we say something was By Accident or On Purpose? What clues help us tell the difference? If we do something by accident, is it still our responsibility?
10 min	Discuss today's activity – building a waterslide. Talk with the group about how to build a waterslide. What features does it need? What can it be made of? etc.
10 min	Player 1 builds a waterslide
10 min	Player 2 continues building waterslide
5 min	Movement Break
10 min	Show other groups the waterslides. What else would be good to add to make a waterpark/playground?
10 min	Player 1 builds playground
10 min	Player 2 builds playground
5 min	Explain Home Challenge and Give Rewards
	Finish

BY ACCIDENT OR ON PURPOSE

Today we learned how to recognize if something has been done by accident or on purpose during the following activities:

○ As a group, we discussed what it means when someone does something By Accident or On Purpose and what to do when we do something by accident. We considered:
  • Apologizing
  • Trying to fix the problem.

○ Working with partners, we designed and built waterslides. We had to:
  • Work together to design the waterslide
  • Encourage our partner
  • Stay calm if someone broke our blocks by accident
  • Apologize and fix it if we broke something by accident.

BY ACCIDENT OR ON PURPOSE

Clues that someone did something <u>On Purpose</u>:

- o The person was looking at you when it happened.

- o The person laughs or smiles after it happened.

- o The person doesn't look concerned or apologize.

Clues that someone did something <u>By Accident</u>:

- o The person was **not** looking at you when it happened.

- o The person looks surprised, embarrassed or sad.

- o The person says 'Sorry' or offers to help.

BY ACCIDENT OR ON PURPOSE

When someone does something <u>On Purpose:</u>

- They wanted to do it.

- They chose to do it.

- They thought about doing it
  before it happened.

When someone does something <u>By Accident:</u>

- They did **not** mean to do it
  or want to do it.

- They did **not** choose
  to do it.

- They did **not** think about
  doing it before it happened.

BY ACCIDENT OR ON PURPOSE

Home Challenge

Which of the examples below are accidents, and which are on purpose? Circle 'A' for Accident or 'P' for On Purpose.

o You are lining up to go into class. The person behind you bumps into you and you fall over. They say sorry and help you up. A / P

o You are playing basketball in the playground. Your ball rolls away from you and another boy picks it up. You ask him to throw it to you, and he throws it to the other side of the playground and laughs. A / P

o You are in art, and the person sitting next to you knocks over a pot of glue. It goes all over your picture and ruins it. They grab some paper towel and try and wipe it off your picture. A / P

SESSION 8: ASKING FOR AND ACCEPTING HELP

World set-up

There are no specific requirements for the world for this session, as students can craft or build items anywhere. Ideally, a world with several different areas or landscapes would be best (e.g. flat area, forest, mountains).

Computer activity

In this session, each student will decide on an object to craft and teach their partner how to build it. Some students may bring ideas from home, or be very familiar with how to make certain items in Minecraft®, while others may need to see a recipe or example to be able to instruct their partner in what to do. It can be useful to have a few books with construction ideas and recipes on hand for the students who are not sure what to build.

For each student's turn on the computer, their partner will be giving instructions on how to build a particular item. Even if the student already knows how to build something, it is important that they listen to their partner and follow directions rather than rushing ahead to finish on their own.

KEY POINTS FOR DISCUSSION

· When might we need to ask others for help? (e.g. when learning something new, when hurt or confused, when something is difficult, etc.)

· How can we ask for help appropriately? – refer to handout

· When someone offers help, how can we accept or refuse their help in a polite way? – refer to handout

· Do others have to accept our help when we offer it?

SKILLS TO HIGHLIGHT DURING THE SESSION

· Listening to partners

· Following instructions

· Asking for and accepting help

· Offering to help others

· Giving compliments

ASKING FOR AND ACCEPTING HELP – SESSION PLAN

Time	Activity
5 min	Welcome
5 min	Review Home Challenge
10 min	Asking For and Accepting Help Talk as a group about when we should ask for help and how to ask appropriately. How should we accept help, or refuse help appropriately if we don't need/want it?
10 min	Discuss today's activity – crafting items. Talk with the group about helping each other to craft or build items. They can craft/build anything they like.
10 min	Player 1 teaches Player 2 how to craft items or build
10 min	Player 2 teaches Player 1 how to craft items or build
5 min	Movement Break
10 min	Discuss what they have created. Was it easy/hard to take instruction from others? How did they help each other with their crafting/building?
10 min	Player 1 Free Play
10 min	Player 2 Free Play
5 min	Explain Home Challenge and Give Rewards
	Finish

ASKING FOR AND ACCEPTING HELP

Today we practised the skills required to Ask For and Accept Help appropriately during the following activities:

○ With the group, we discussed when and how we should ask for help. We then talked about how to accept or refuse help when it is offered.

○ Working on the computers, we took turns helping our partners to craft or build items of our choice. We had to:

- Decide what to craft/build
- Break down the task into steps
- Listen and follow instructions
- Be patient
- Encourage our partners and compliment their efforts.

95

ASKING FOR AND ACCEPTING HELP

How to Ask for Help appropriately:

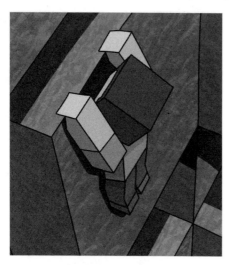

Could you please
help me?

I didn't understand the
instructions. Could you
please tell me again?

Would you please
show me what to do?

ASKING FOR AND ACCEPTING HELP

How to Accept or Refuse Help appropriately:

Thanks. I'll give it a try.

Thanks. That's a good idea.

Thanks. But I can do it myself.

Thanks. But I'd like to try it my way.

ASKING FOR AND ACCEPTING HELP

Home Challenge

When we are trying something for the first time or learning something new, we often need some help.

o Write down four things you needed help to learn.

1. _____
2. _____
3. _____
4. _____

o Think of three people you can ask for help when you need it. Write their names in the spaces below.

1. _____
2. _____
3. _____

SESSION 9: HOW OUR BEHAVIOUR IMPACTS OTHERS

World set-up

There are no specific requirements for the world for this session, as students can craft or build items anywhere. Ideally, a world with several different areas or landscapes would be best (e.g. flat area, forest, mountains).

Computer activity

In this session, students will create 'machines' or cause-and-effect devices using Redstone. Some students may bring ideas from home, or be very familiar with how to make certain items in Minecraft®, while others may need to see a recipe or example to be able to construct an object. It can be useful to have a few books with construction ideas and recipes for using Redstone on hand for the students who are not sure what to build.

Group activity

During the second group discussion time, students are encouraged to create a story as a group using Minecraft® characters to illustrate how behaviour can impact others. I find it easiest to have a white board or butcher's paper on hand, and have the students contribute ideas for an event in the story and what will happen next, while I write the sequence of events down. The facilitator may need to prompt ideas to bring the story to a close if it is going for too long. Ideally, the facilitator will type up the story (with pictures if possible) and provide each of the students with a copy at the next session.

KEY POINTS FOR DISCUSSION

- What does 'cause and effect' mean?

- What does it mean when we say that behaviour has consequences?

- Can you think of situations where something positive or negative has happened due to your behaviour?

- Why is it important to think about the impact of our behaviour on others before we say or do something?

- What could the impact of Steve's behaviour be on the Creeper? – refer to handout (e.g. Steve sees a Creeper – Steve waves and says hello – Steve and the Creeper become friends *or* Steve sees a Creeper – Steve tries to attack the Creeper – the Creeper comes after Steve)

SKILLS TO HIGHLIGHT DURING THE SESSION

- Managing impulses appropriately
- Using nice words
- Being considerate of others
- Helping others

HOW OUR BEHAVIOUR IMPACTS OTHERS – SESSION PLAN

Time	Activity
5 min	Welcome
5 min	Review Home Challenge
10 min	Talk as a group about how our choices and Behaviour Impact Others – positive impact/negative impact. What does cause and effect mean?
10 min	Discuss today's activity – use Redstone recipes to create working machines
10 min	Player 1 crafts with Redstone
10 min	Player 2 crafts with Redstone
5 min	Movement Break
10 min	Make up a Minecraft® story together as a group. Consider the impact each action taken in the story has on the other characters
10 min	Player 1 continues to craft with Redstone
10 min	Player 2 continues to craft with Redstone
5 min	Explain Home Challenge and Give Rewards
	Finish

HOW OUR BEHAVIOUR IMPACTS OTHERS

Today we learned about how our choices and Behaviour Impacts Others during the following activities:

o With the group, we discussed what consequences are and how what we do and say impacts other people.

o Working with partners, we made devices using Redstone, which involves considering cause and effect.

o As a group, we developed a story based on Minecraft®, and discussed the actions of the characters and how they would impact each other.

HOW OUR BEHAVIOUR IMPACTS OTHERS

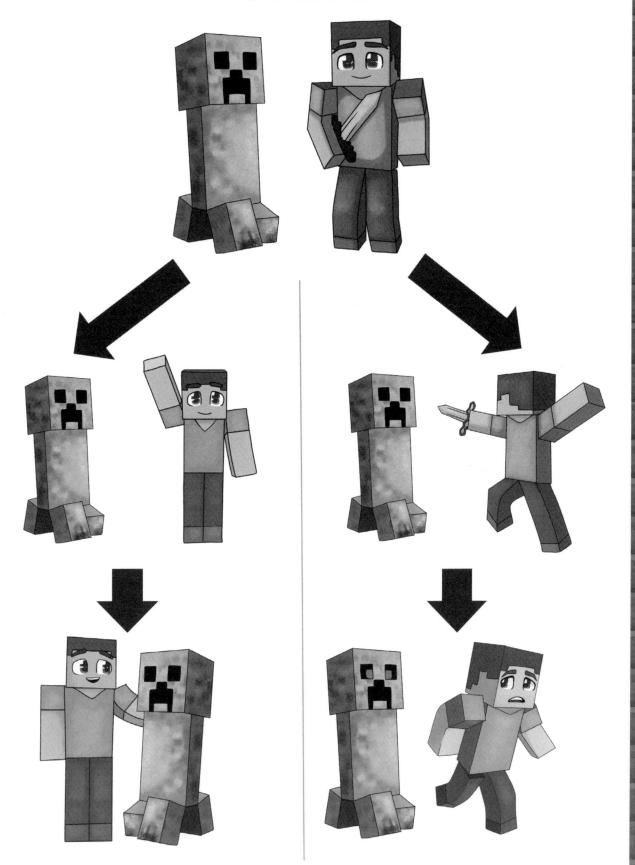

HOW OUR BEHAVIOUR IMPACTS OTHERS

Home Challenge

For each example below, think about whether the first person's behaviour would have a positive or negative impact on the second person. Place a tick in the correct column.

	Positive	Negative
Sam takes the ball Ally is playing with.		✓
Josh frowns and looks away when Tom says 'Hello'.		
Alecia shares her coloured pencils with Josh.		
Jack helps Sally with her maths worksheet.		
Cody pushes Harry to get to the front of the line.		
Zoe helps Cooper pick up the books he dropped.		
Sean blows up Tom's castle in Minecraft®.		
Tim helps Alecia up when she trips and falls over.		
Ally laughs when Cooper's lunch spills on the ground.		

SESSION 10: PUTTING IT ALL TOGETHER – SUMMARY SESSION

World set-up

The world for this session is ideally flat to allow room for the students to construct houses for their village.

Computer activity

Students will construct houses to create a village in Minecraft® this session. As a group, students should discuss what types of houses or buildings are needed in a village, what materials they might use, who will build what type of building, and where they will build.

KEY POINTS FOR DISCUSSION

- Why is it important to consider another person's point of view?

- How can we recognize when someone does something by accident or on purpose?

- What is the best way to ask for help when we need it and accept or refuse help appropriately?

- How can our behaviour impact on others at school and at home?

SKILLS TO HIGHLIGHT DURING THE SESSION

- Accepting other opinions and points of view

- Using nice words

- Asking for and offering help appropriately

- Accepting help from others

- Staying calm when something happens by accident

PUTTING IT ALL TOGETHER – SESSION PLAN

Time	Activity
5 min	Welcome
5 min	Review Home Challenge
10 min	What have we learned about this week? o Another Point of View o By Accident or On Purpose o Asking For and Accepting Help o How Our Behaviour Impacts Others Talk as a group about what we have learned and how we can use this information at school and at home.
10 min	Discuss today's activity – making a village. Decide as a group what buildings we need, who will build what and where, etc.
10 min	Player 1 builds in the village
10 min	Player 2 builds in the village
5 min	Movement Break
10 min	Discuss what they have created. Was it easy/hard? How did they use the skills they have learned this week?
10 min	Player 1 builds village or Free Play
10 min	Player 2 builds village or Free Play
5 min	Give Certificates and Rewards
	Finish

PUTTING IT ALL TOGETHER

Today we reviewed and practised the skills we have learned over the last few sessions during the following activities:

o With the group, we discussed what we have learned and how we can use these skills at home and at school.

o Working as a team, we made a village in Minecraft®. We had to:

- Consider others' POINTS OF VIEW
- Understand and accept when others' do things BY ACCIDENT
- ASK FOR and ACCEPT HELP
- Have a POSITIVE IMPACT on others' behaviour.

SESSION 11: HAVING A CONVERSATION

World set-up

For this session, the world should be flat or at least have some flat areas so students can build their houses.

Computer activity

The main activity for this session is to create gingerbread houses. These can be made out of any materials. Students should be encouraged to use different colours and textures to create the look of a gingerbread house.

KEY POINTS FOR DISCUSSION

- What are good communication skills? – refer to handout

- What does having a conversation with someone involve?

- What topics are good to have a conversation about?

- Are there any topics it is best not to talk about with others?

- How do you find interests you share with someone else? – refer to handout

- Why is it good to talk to your friends about shared interests?

SKILLS TO HIGHLIGHT DURING THE SESSION

- Taking turns to talk

- Staying on topic

- Looking at the person who is talking

- Making comments and asking questions

HAVING A CONVERSATION – SESSION PLAN

Time	Activity
5 min	Welcome and Introductions
10 min	Group Rules and Minecraft® money
10 min	Having a Conversation Discuss and review as a group what qualities make good communication skills.
5 min	Discuss today's activity – building a gingerbread house. Talk with the group about what features a gingerbread house needs, what it can be made of, etc.
10 min	Player 1 builds a gingerbread house with Player 2's help
10 min	Player 2 builds a gingerbread house with Player 1's help
5 min	Movement Break
5 min	Discuss as a group what topics are good to have conversations about. Introduce the idea of 'shared interests'. Use real examples from the kids to find topics that would be 'shared interests' for different people (e.g. friends, parents, siblings, etc.).
5 min	Find topics that are 'shared interests' between Player 1 and Player 2
10 min	Player 1 continues to build or free play
10 min	Player 2 continues to build or free play
5 min	Explain Home Challenge and Give Rewards
	Finish

HAVING A CONVERSATION

Today we learned about what makes a good Conversation during the following activities:

o With the group, we reviewed what good communication skills are.

o We practised our communication skills while helping our partners build a gingerbread house.

o With the group we learned about how we can find topics to talk about that our friends are also interested in.

o Then we practised our conversation skills by finding topics in common with our partners and talking about them.

HAVING A CONVERSATION

Review: What are good communication skills?

Start or end the conversation.
Say 'Hello' or 'Goodbye'.

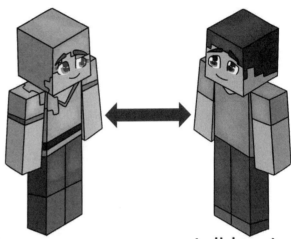

Look at the person you are talking to.
Turn your body towards the person.

Ask and answer questions.
Listen to what is being said.

Take turns to talk.
Talk about the same thing.

HAVING A CONVERSATION

Finding shared interests:

Steve likes:
Mining
Trains
Creepers
Building

SHARED INTERESTS

?

Alex likes:
Horses
Diamonds
Zombies
Mining

Topics that Steve and Alex both like are 'shared interests' and would be good to talk about.

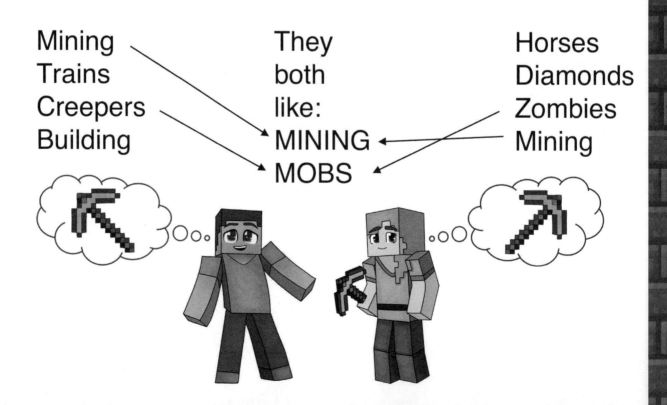

Mining
Trains
Creepers
Building

They both like:
MINING
MOBS

Horses
Diamonds
Zombies
Mining

HAVING A CONVERSATION

Home Challenge

Shared interests:

o Think about topics that you are interested in and also what interests a friend or member of your family.

o Fill in the diagram below, putting interests that both you and your friend or family member share in the talking bubble in the centre.

o Try having a conversation about one of your **shared interests**.

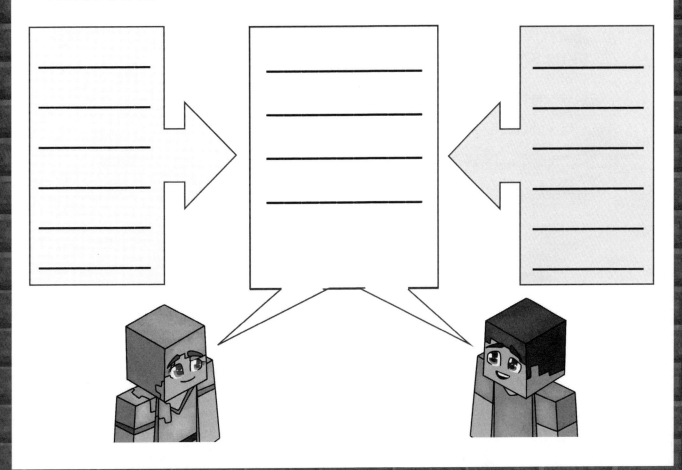

SESSION 12: BEING ASSERTIVE

World set-up

In this session, the world needs to be flat or feature large open spaces, to enable students to create giant robots.

Computer activity

For the activity this session, students will design and build giant robots. They should be encouraged to be creative and use their imaginations, and to use whatever materials interest them.

Before moving to the computers, students should discuss as a group what kinds of features and materials could be used for building their robot. Then in pairs, students can further discuss their individual designs before starting work on the computers.

KEY POINTS FOR DISCUSSION

- What do we mean when we say someone is assertive?

- Why is being assertive better than being passive or aggressive?

- What does being assertive look like/sound like? – refer to handout

- How might others feel if you are aggressive towards them?

SKILLS TO HIGHLIGHT DURING THE SESSION

- Taking turns to talk

- Communicating in an assertive way

- Offering and accepting help

BEING ASSERTIVE – SESSION PLAN

Time	Activity
5 min	Welcome
5 min	Review Group Rules and Home Challenge
10 min	What do we mean when we say someone is Assertive? Why is being assertive better than being passive or aggressive? What does being assertive look like/sound like?
10 min	Discuss today's activity – making a giant robot. Talk with the group about what features a robot might need? What can it be made of? How high should it be? etc.
5 min	Plan robot with partner
10 min	Player 1 builds a robot
10 min	Player 2 continues to build a robot
5 min	Movement Break
5 min	Show other groups the robots. What else would be good to add? How can you let others know you like their robot?
10 min	Player 1 continues to build robot or Free Play
10 min	Player 2 continues to build robot or Free Play
5 min	Explain Home Challenge and Give Rewards
	Finish

BEING ASSERTIVE

Today we learned how to be Assertive in our interactions with others during the following activities:

- ○ As a group, we discussed what it means when someone is assertive rather than aggressive or passive. We considered why it is good to be assertive, and how assertive people look, talk and behave.

- ○ Working with partners, we designed and built giant robots. We had to:
  - Work together to design the robot
  - Encourage our partner
  - Communicate in an assertive way
  - Find a compromise if we disagreed with our partner.

BEING ASSERTIVE

ASSERTIVE

o Calm
o Strong
o In control
o Use manners
o Speak up
o Make eye contact
o Stand up straight

AGGRESSIVE

o Angry
o Tense
o Threatening
o Bossy
o Loud
o Stares
o Stands close

PASSIVE

o Quiet
o Shy
o Nervous
o Picked on
o Bossed around
o Look down
o Don't speak up

BEING ASSERTIVE

Home Challenge

Think about some characters you know from TV, movies and games that you would describe as Assertive, Passive or Aggressive.

List at least one character that fits each of the descriptions below.

ASSERTIVE

1. _____   2. _____

3. _____   4. _____

PASSIVE

1. _____   2. _____

3. _____   4. _____

AGGRESSIVE

1. _____   2. _____

3. _____   4. _____

SESSION 13: BEING PERSISTENT

World set-up

For this session, the world needs to have plenty of water in which to build submarines. An island or a location close to an ocean would be ideal.

Computer activity

In this session, students will design and build their own submarines. These can be built completely submerged in water, or on the surface, and can be created using any materials. It could be helpful to provide pictures of a few different submarines for students who are unsure of what a submarine should look like.

KEY POINTS FOR DISCUSSION

- What is persistence? – refer to handout

- Why is it important to be persistent?

- How do you feel when you make a mistake?

- Why should you keep trying if you don't get something right the first time?

- What is something you learned to do after persisting until you achieved it? (e.g. riding a bike, writing with a pen, learning a dance move, building an Ender portal in Minecraft®, etc.)

SKILLS TO HIGHLIGHT DURING THE SESSION

- Persisting to complete a task

- Encouraging others

- Problem solving

BEING PERSISTENT – SESSION PLAN

Time	Activity
5 min	Welcome
5 min	Review Home Challenge
10 min	Talk as a group about what being Persistent means and why it is important. How do you feel when you make mistakes? Why should you keep trying if you don't do something right the first time? Or the second time? What have you learned/achieved after persisting for a while?
5 min	Discuss today's activity – building a submarine. Talk with the group about how to build a submarine, what features to include, etc.
5 min	Talk with your partner about what you would like your submarine to look like.
10 min	Player 1 builds a submarine
10 min	Player 2 builds a submarine
5 min	Movement Break
10 min	Discuss what was easy/hard for them. What happened when you kept trying/persisted? What other objects would you like to be able to make in Minecraft®?
10 min	Player 1 Free Play
10 min	Player 2 Free Play
5 min	Explain Home Challenge and Give Rewards
	Finish

BEING PERSISTENT

Today we practised the skills required to be Persistent when something is difficult, while completing the following activities:

o With the group, we discussed what it means to be persistent and how persisting when things get difficult helps us learn and develop new skills.

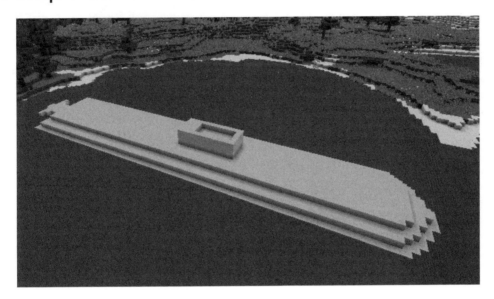

o Working on the computers, we took turns building a submarine. We had to:

- Create a design
- Break down the task into steps
- Stay calm
- Encourage our partners and compliment their efforts
- Keep trying when things got difficult
- Ask for help if needed.

BEING PERSISTENT

Stay calm

Keep trying

Ask for help

Don't give up

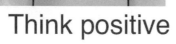

Think positive

BEING PERSISTENT

Home Challenge

Think about a time when you found something difficult but kept trying (persisted) until you could do it, then answer the following questions:

1. What were you trying to do?

_____

_____

2. How did you feel when you were finding it hard?

_____

_____

3. What happened when you kept trying?

_____

_____

_____

4. How did you feel when you could do it?

_____

_____

_____

SESSION 14: MANAGING CONFLICT

World set-up

For this session, the world should be flat or at least have some flat areas so students can build their playgrounds on an open area.

Computer activity

The activity for this session is to create a playground. Each student will need to find an area to build on and to decide on what kinds of equipment they will feature (e.g. swings, slide, climbing fort).

KEY POINTS FOR DISCUSSION

- What is conflict?

- What kinds of situations can cause conflict with others?

- Who might you experience conflict with at home or school?

- What is the best way to manage conflict? – refer to handout

SKILLS TO HIGHLIGHT DURING THE SESSION

- Sharing ideas with others

- Taking turns to talk

- Staying calm when there is a conflict with a peer

- Asking for and offering help

MANAGING CONFLICT – SESSION PLAN

Time	Activity
5 min	Welcome
5 min	Review Home Challenge
10 min	What is Conflict? Talk as a group about what conflict is. What are some examples of conflict they might have with peers, siblings and adults? What are some good/not good ways to manage conflict?
10 min	Discuss today's activity – creating a playground. Talk with the group about what the playground could include. Discuss materials, equipment, etc.
5 min	Design playground
10 min	Player 1 builds playground
10 min	Player 2 builds playground
5 min	Movement Break
5 min	Discuss what features they have included in their playgrounds
10 min	Player 1 continues to build playground or Free Play
10 min	Player 2 continues to build playground or Free Play
5 min	Explain Home Challenge and Give Rewards
	Finish

MANAGING CONFLICT

Today we discussed and practised the skills required to Manage Conflict with others during the following activities:

○ With the group we discussed what conflict is, what causes conflict and what we should do when a conflict happens with family or friends.

○ Working with partners, we built playgrounds in Minecraft®. We had to:
- Design a playground
- Choose materials and equipment
- Find a good place to build
- Appropriately manage any conflict about where to build, materials used, whose turn was next and others trying to help.

MANAGING CONFLICT

What is the best way to Manage Conflict with others?

Stay calm

Use your words

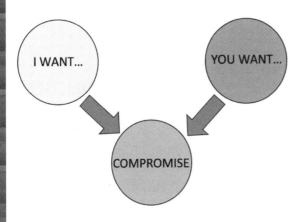

Be assertive

Listen to others

Compromise

Ask for help

MANAGING CONFLICT

Home Challenge

○ Write down two examples of conflicts you have had with others at school or at home.

1. _____

2. _____

○ What would you do if a child pushed in front of you in the line to go outside?

_____

_____

_____

○ What would you do if a child was calling you names in the playground?

_____

_____

_____

SESSION 15: PUTTING IT ALL TOGETHER – SUMMARY SESSION

World set-up

There are no specific requirements for the world for this session, as students can build their castles in any location. Ideally, a world with several different areas or landscapes would be best (e.g. flat area, forest, mountains).

Computer activity

For this session, students will design and build a castle. Students should discuss the features and materials required with their partners, and find suitable locations for them to build separately or together before going on the computers.

KEY POINTS FOR DISCUSSION

- What is good communication?

- How do we have a conversation with others about shared interest?

- What does being assertive look/sound like?

- Why is it important to be persistent and keep trying when something is difficult?

- How do we manage conflict with others appropriately?

SKILLS TO HIGHLIGHT DURING THE SESSION

- Communicating clearly and assertively

- Talking about shared interests

- Persistence with challenging tasks

- Asking for help

- Staying calm when there is conflict with a peer

PUTTING IT ALL TOGETHER – SESSION PLAN

Time	Activity
5 min	Welcome
5 min	Review Home Challenge
10 min	What have we learned about this week? o Having a Conversation o Being Assertive o Being Persistent o Managing Conflict Talk as a group about what we have learned and how we can use this information at school and at home.
10 min	Discuss today's activity – making a castle. Decide in pairs what materials are needed, who will build what and where, etc.
10 min	Player 1 builds a castle
10 min	Player 2 builds a castle
5 min	Movement Break
10 min	Discuss what they have created. Was it easy/hard? How did they use the skills they have learned this week?
10 min	Player 1 builds castle or Free Play
10 min	Player 2 builds castle or Free Play
5 min	Give Certificates and Rewards
	Finish

PUTTING IT ALL TOGETHER

Today we reviewed and practised the skills we have learned over the last few sessions during the following activities:

o With the group, we discussed what we have learned and how we can use these skills at home and at school.

o Working with partners, we made a castle in Minecraft®. We had to:
- COMMUNICATE our ideas in an ASSERTIVE way
- Keep trying and be PERSISTENT if the activity became difficult
- MANAGE CONFLICT if we had a disagreement with our partner
- Have a CONVERSATION with others about what we built.

SESSION 16: SHOWING INTEREST IN OTHERS

World set-up

There are no specific requirements for the world for this session, as students can build their underground hideouts in any location. Ideally, a world with several different areas or landscapes would be best (e.g. flat area, forest, mountains).

Computer activity

In this session, students will build secret underground hideouts. Hideouts can be built by digging into the ground or the side of a mountain, or using an existing cave as a starting point. Encourage students to find ways of hiding the entrance to their hideout and consider what features a hideout would need inside.

KEY POINTS FOR DISCUSSION

- Why is it important to show interest in our friends?

- How do you feel when your friends show interest in you?

- How can we show others we are interested in them?

- What is active listening? – refer to handout

- How can we use active listening to show interest in our friends?

SKILLS TO HIGHLIGHT DURING THE SESSION

- Showing interest in others

- Active listening

- Asking for and offering help

- Using nice words

SHOWING INTEREST IN OTHERS – SESSION PLAN

Time	Activity
5 min	Welcome and Introductions
5 min	Group Rules and Minecraft® money
10 min	Showing Interest in Others Discuss as a group why it is important to show interest in others and brainstorm how we can show others we are interested in them.
5 min	Discuss today's activity – building an underground hideout. Talk with the group about what features a hideout needs, what it can be made of, etc.
10 min	Player 1 builds an underground hideout
10 min	Player 2 builds an underground hideout
5 min	Movement Break
10 min	Active Listening Learn about and practise active listening as a way to show interest in others.
5 min	Discuss ideas and improvements for hideouts with partners
10 min	Player 1 continues building hideout
10 min	Player 2 continues building hideout
5 min	Explain Home Challenge and Give Rewards
	Finish

SHOWING INTEREST IN OTHERS

Today we learned how to Show Interest in Others and why it is important during the following activities:

o With the group, we discussed the different ways we can show interest in others.

o We practised showing interest in others while discussing ideas and building a secret underground hideout with our partners.

o With the group we learned about 'Active Listening' and how we can use it to show others we are interested in them.

o With our partners, we practised our 'Active Listening' skills while talking about our hideouts and making improvements.

SHOWING INTEREST IN OTHERS

Active Listening:

Stop what you are doing

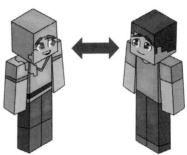

Look at the person who is speaking

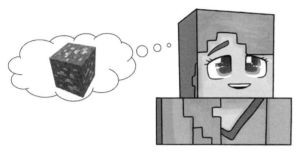

Focus on what they are saying

Listen without interrupting

Ask for more information

Give positive feedback

Don't steal the spotlight

SHOWING INTEREST IN OTHERS

Active Listening:

1. Stop what you are doing.

   o Don't fidget or be distracted by other activities.

2. Look at the person who is speaking.

   o Turn your body to the person and look at their face.

3. Focus on what they are saying.

   o Think about what the person is saying.

   o Don't let your mind wander.

4. Listen without interrupting.

   o Don't speak until they pause and give you a chance to say something.

5. Ask for more information.

   o Ask a question about something the person has said.

6. Give positive feedback.

   o Make a comment.

   o Use body language.

7. Don't steal the spotlight.

   o Keep the focus on the person who is speaking.

   o Don't talk about yourself.

SHOWING INTEREST IN OTHERS

Home Challenge

Active Listening:

- Ask a family member or friend about how their weekend was and practise your active listening skills.

- Remember: focus on the person and what they are saying; listen without interrupting, ask for more information, make a comment or give feedback. Don't steal the spotlight by talking about you, this is their chance to shine!

- Write down two pieces of information your friend or family member shared on the lines below:

1. _____
_____
_____

2. _____
_____
_____

SESSION 17: USING YOUR SOCIAL FILTER

World set-up

For this session, the world should be flat or at least have some flat areas so students can build their self-portraits in an open area.

Computer activity

In this session, students will create a self-portrait with pixel art. Students can use any materials in their inventory to access the coloured blocks they need and create a 2-D representation of themselves. Self-portraits may feature just a student's face, or a full body image, depending on the preference of the student.

KEY POINTS FOR DISCUSSION

- How do you know what is appropriate to say in social situations?

- What is your social filter?

- Why is it important to use your social filter when talking to others?

- How do others feel when you say something that is not appropriate?

- What are the four steps for using your social filter effectively? – refer to handout

SKILLS TO HIGHLIGHT DURING THE SESSION

- Talking about shared interests

- Considering the feelings of others before saying something

- Giving compliments

USING YOUR SOCIAL FILTER – SESSION PLAN

Time	Activity
5 min	Welcome
5 min	Review Group Rules and Home Challenge
10 min	What is your Social Filter? Talk as a group about how we know what is OK/not OK to say in social situations. Brainstorm what is OK to talk about and what is not OK.
5 min	Discuss today's activity – making a self-portrait in pixel art. Talk with the group about what materials will they use, what features to include, etc.
10 min	Player 1 creates self-portrait
10 min	Player 2 creates self-portrait
5 min	Movement Break
5 min	Discuss what features they included in their portraits
10 min	Talk as a group about four steps to help us use our social filter and say the right thing.
10 min	Player 1 pixel art or Free Play
10 min	Player 2 pixel art or Free Play
5 min	Explain Home Challenge and Give Rewards
	Finish

USING YOUR SOCIAL FILTER

Today we learned about using our Social Filter during the following activities:

o With the group, we discussed how we need our social filter to help us make good choices in social situations.

o We practised using our social filter while we created self-portraits with pixel art and talked about what we had made with our partners.

o With the group we learned about the four steps our social filter needs to go through to help us make good choices in social situations:
- Stop
- Think
- Decide
- Choose.

USING YOUR SOCIAL FILTER

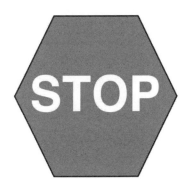

STOP what you are doing.

THINK about what you are going to say.

DECIDE which words need to stay in your head, and which can be said out loud.

CHOOSE words that are kind, friendly and helpful to say out loud.

USING YOUR SOCIAL FILTER

Home Challenge

We all have times when we forget to use our social filter.

Think about a situation where you didn't use your social filter and someone became upset or angry.

What did you say?

_____

_____

_____

How did the people around you react?

_____

_____

_____

If you had used your social filter, what could you have said or done that would have made the situation better?

_____

_____

_____

SESSION 18: FOLLOWING THE RULES

World set-up

There are no specific requirements for the world for this session, as students can build their towers in any location. Ideally, a world with several different areas or landscapes would be best (e.g. flat area, forest, mountains).

Computer activity

Students will build towers to particular specifications for the computer activity for this session. The specifications are up to the facilitator to set, but should include a few details that have to be featured in the tower. The main point of the task is that students follow any rules set by the facilitator. Specifications could include details such as the number of windows, building materials, the height or width of the tower, or decorations.

KEY POINTS FOR DISCUSSION

- What places/situations have rules that you need to follow?

- What happens when you don't follow a rule at home or at school?

- Why do we have rules and why are they important to follow? – refer to handout

- How do you feel when others don't follow the rules?

- What is expected and unexpected behaviour? – refer to handout

- What happens when you behave in an unexpected way?

SKILLS TO HIGHLIGHT DURING THE SESSION

- Following the rules

- Using nice rules

- Listening to others

- Taking turns to talk

FOLLOWING THE RULES – SESSION PLAN

Time	Activity
5 min	Welcome
5 min	Review Home Challenge
10 min	Talk as a group about why we have rules and why it is important to Follow the Rules. What places/situations have rules that you need to follow? What happens when you don't follow a rule at home/at school/in a game? Why are rules important? Why do we need them? How do you feel when other people don't follow the rules?
10 min	Discuss today's activity – building a tower. Talk with the group about building their tower to specific requirements.
10 min	Player 1 builds a tower
10 min	Player 1 builds a tower
5 min	Movement Break
10 min	Discuss whether it was easy/hard for them to follow the rules. Are some rules easier to follow than others? Introduce concept of Expected vs Unexpected Behaviour
10 min	Player 1 Free Play
10 min	Player 2 Free Play
5 min	Explain Home Challenge and Give Rewards
	Finish

FOLLOWING THE RULES

Today we learned about why we have rules and practised Following Rules, while completing the following activities:

o With the group, we discussed why rules are important and what types of situations we need to have rules for.

o Working on the computers, we took turns building a tower using specific rules about the size, materials and decoration.

o With the group we discussed the concept of Expected and Unexpected behaviour and the impact of Unexpected behaviour on others.

FOLLOWING THE RULES

Why do we need rules?

To keep us safe

To keep others safe

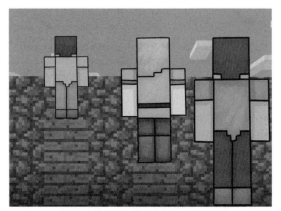

To make things fair

To help us play

To help us make
good choices

FOLLOWING THE RULES

Expected vs Unexpected Behaviour

Expected Behaviours:

- o Are behaviours that are appropriate according to social rules.

- o Are friendly, polite or respectful.

- o Make people feel happy and calm.

Unexpected Behaviours:

- o Do not follow social rules.

- o Are rude, disrespectful or inappropriate.

- o Make people feel sad, uncomfortable or angry.

FOLLOWING THE RULES

Home Challenge

Think about the kinds of rules you have to follow at school and at home.

On the lines below, write down two rules (one from school and one from home) and the reason you need to follow them.

Rule 1:

_____

_____

Reason for Rule 1:

_____

_____

Rule 2:

_____

_____

Reason for Rule 2:

_____

_____

SESSION 19: PROBLEM SOLVING

World set-up

There are no specific requirements for the world for this session, as students can build their sky houses in any location. Ideally, a world with several different areas or landscapes would be best (e.g. flat area, forest, mountains).

Computer activity

In this session, students will build a floating village in the sky. Before going to the computers, the group should discuss the features that are important to include in their sky houses, and where they could be built. To make a house float in the sky, students will first need to build a tower of single blocks to the height they want, then build their house on top of it. Once their house is finished, they can destroy the blocks of the tower and the house will float.

KEY POINTS FOR DISCUSSION

- What is a problem?

- What kinds of problems do you experience at home and at school?

- How can we solve problems? What are some good/not good ways of solving problems?

- What are the five steps for problem solving? – refer to handout

SKILLS TO HIGHLIGHT DURING THE SESSION

- Working together

- Using nice words

- Using problem-solving skills

- Taking turns to talk

PROBLEM SOLVING – SESSION PLAN

Time	Activity
5 min	Welcome
5 min	Review Home Challenge
10 min	What is Problem Solving? Talk as a group about what problem solving is and when we might use it. What are some examples of problems that we need to solve? What are some good/not good ways to solve problems?
5 min	Discuss today's activity - making a house in a floating village in the sky. Decide in pairs what materials are needed, who will build what and where, etc.
5 min	Design a sky house
10 min	Player 1 builds a sky house
10 min	Player 2 builds a sky house
5 min	Movement Break
5 min	Discuss what features they have included in their sky house
5 min	Introduce Five Steps for Problem Solving
10 min	Player 1 continues to build a sky house or Free Play
10 min	Player 2 continues to build a sky house or Free Play
5 min	Explain Home Challenge and Give Rewards
	Finish

PROBLEM SOLVING

Today we discussed and practised the skills required to solve problems during the following activities:

○ With the group we discussed what problem solving is, and the kinds of problems we might need to solve at school and at home.

○ Working with partners, we built floating houses in the sky.

○ With the group we learned about the Five Steps for Problem Solving and how we can use these steps to solve problems in our everyday lives.

PROBLEM SOLVING

Five Steps for Problem Solving:

Identify the problem

Brainstorm solutions

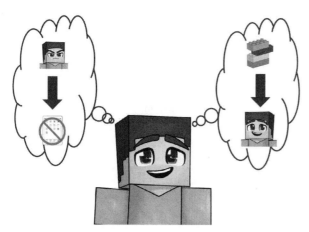

Think – what would happen if…?

Decide on an action

Ask yourself – was it successful?

PROBLEM SOLVING

Home Challenge

Use the Five Steps for Problem Solving to solve a real problem you have experienced at home or at school.

Identify the problem

Brainstorm solutions			
1.	2.	3.	4.

What would happen if…?			
1.	2.	3.	4.

Decide on an action

Was it successful?

SESSION 20: PUTTING IT ALL TOGETHER – SUMMARY SESSION

World set-up

For this session, the world should be flat or at least have some flat areas so students can build their bedrooms.

Computer activity

In this activity, students will recreate their bedrooms in the Minecraft® world. Students can use any materials in their inventory to create a model of their bedroom, including important features, colour schemes and furniture.

KEY POINTS FOR DISCUSSION

· What is active listening?

· Why do we need to use our social filter when we talk to other people?

· What places/situations do you have to follow rules?

· Why do we need rules?

· How can we use the five steps to problem solving?

SKILLS TO HIGHLIGHT DURING THE SESSION

· Showing interest in others

· Using nice words

· Making appropriate comments

· Following the group rules

· Problem solving when things go wrong

PUTTING IT ALL TOGETHER – SESSION PLAN

Time	Activity
5 min	Welcome
5 min	Review Home Challenge
10 min	What have we learned about this week? ○ Showing Interest in Others ○ Using your Social Filter ○ Following the Rules ○ Problem Solving Talk as a group about what we have learned and how we can use this information at school and at home.
10 min	Discuss today's activity – recreating your bedroom in Minecraft®. Decide in pairs what materials are needed, who will build what and where, etc.
10 min	Player 1 builds their bedroom
10 min	Player 2 builds their bedroom
5 min	Movement Break
5 min	Discuss what they have created. Was it easy/hard? How did they use the skills they have learned this week?
10 min	Player 1 builds bedroom or Free Play
10 min	Player 2 builds bedroom or Free Play
10 min	Give Certificates and Rewards
	Finish

PUTTING IT ALL TOGETHER

Today we reviewed and practised the skills we have learned over the last few sessions during the following activities:

o With the group, we discussed what we have learned and how we can use these skills at home and at school.

o Working with partners, we recreated our bedrooms in Minecraft®. We had to:

- SHOW INTEREST in the ideas of our partners
- Use our SOCIAL FILTERS to communicate in an appropriate way
- FOLLOW THE GROUP RULES to keep everyone safe and happy
- Use our PROBLEM-SOLVING skills to manage problems that occurred with our partners or while creating our bedrooms.

SESSION 21: TONE OF VOICE

World set-up

For this session, the world should be flat or at least have some flat areas so students can build spaceships in an open location.

Computer activity

Students will design and build spaceships during this session. These can be built on the ground or in the air, and can be created using any materials. It could be helpful to provide pictures of a few different spaceships for students who are unsure of what a spaceship should look like.

KEY POINTS FOR DISCUSSION

· What do we mean when we talk about 'tone of voice'? – refer to handout

· How does our tone of voice change when we are angry/excited/sad?

· How do you feel when someone's tone of voice and words don't match?

· What can you do if a person's tone of voice and words don't match? – refer to handout

SKILLS TO HIGHLIGHT DURING THE SESSION

· Appropriate tone of voice

· Using nice words

· Asking for and offering help

· Taking turns to talk

TONE OF VOICE – SESSION PLAN

Time	Activity
5 min	Welcome and Introductions
5 min	Group Rules and Minecraft® money
10 min	Tone of Voice Discuss as a group what we mean by 'tone of voice' and how our tone of voice can change the meaning of the words we use (e.g. volume, pitch, emotion).
5 min	Discuss today's activity – creating a spaceship. Talk with the group about what features a spaceship needs, what it can be made of, etc.
5 min	Design your own spaceship. Talk to your partner about your ideas
10 min	Player 1 builds their spaceship
10 min	Player 2 builds their spaceship
5 min	Movement Break
5 min	Tone of Voice What can we do if someone's words don't match their tone of voice?
5 min	Discuss ideas and improvements for spaceships with partners
10 min	Player 1 continues building spaceship and adds features (e.g. aliens, planets) or Free Play
10 min	Player 2 continues building spaceship and adds features (e.g. aliens, planets) or Free Play
5 min	Explain Home Challenge and Give Rewards
	Finish

TONE OF VOICE

Today we learned about different Tones of Voice and why it is important to be aware of the tone of voice (e.g. volume and pitch) we use when speaking to others during the following activities:

o With the group, we discussed the different ways we can use our tone of voice to communicate with others and how our tone of voice can change the meaning of our words.

o We practised using an appropriate tone of voice while discussing ideas and building spaceships with our partners.

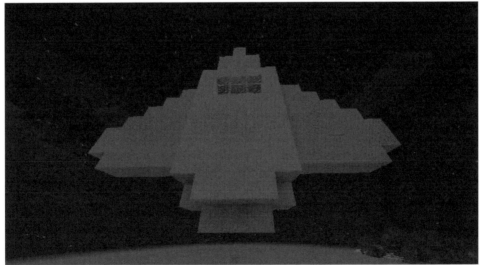

o With the group we learned about what we can do if someone's tone of voice doesn't match the words they are using.

TONE OF VOICE

Remember: The way we speak changes the meaning of our words.

When you talk to others, think about your voice VOLUME and PITCH and EMOTION.

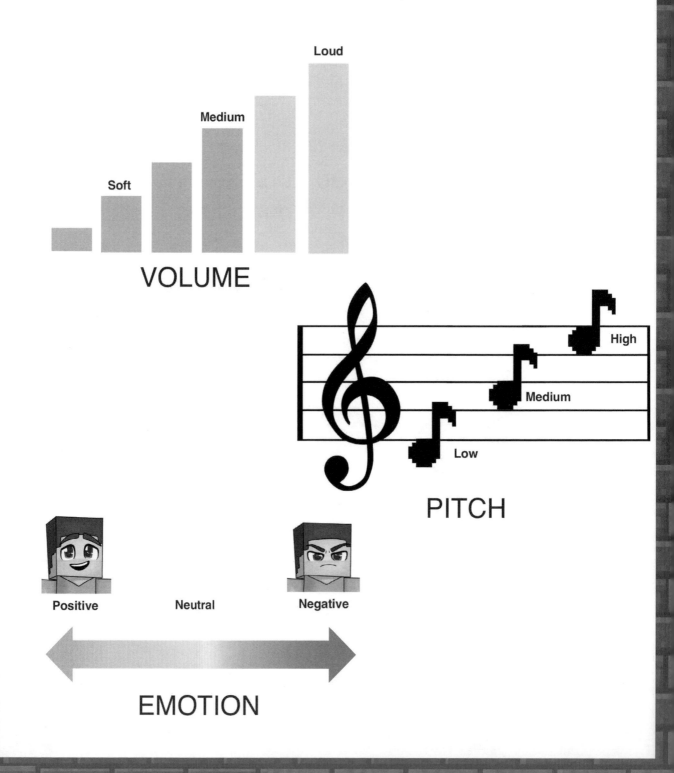

TONE OF VOICE

When a person's Tone of Voice and words don't match:

1. Look at the person's body language.
   o What clues are they giving with their facial expression and body?

2. Look at the situation.
   o Where are you?
   o What is happening around you?
   o What was the person doing before they spoke to you?

3. Ask a question.
   o If you are still not sure how the person is feeling, ask them.
   o 'I'm sorry but I can't read your tone of voice. Are you upset?'
   o 'You sound a bit angry. Is there something wrong?'

161

TONE OF VOICE

Home Challenge

With a family member, try saying the following statements and questions with the emotions in brackets next to them.

1. I love ice cream. (bored, happy)

2. I have so much homework. (excited, worried)

3. I really like your hat. (annoyed, happy)

4. Why can't I go too? (sad, surprised)

5. I can do it myself. (angry, friendly)

Does the meaning of the words change when you say them with a different tone of voice?

SESSION 22: SIZE OF THE PROBLEM

World set-up

For this session, a flat world will be required. You will need to spend some time before the session creating a maze. The maze can be built using any materials in the inventory and can be as simple or complex as you like.

If you require assistance with creating the maze, there are a number of free online maze generators that can be used to create a template to follow when creating the maze in Minecraft®.

Computer activity

For the first computer activity in this session, students will find their way through the maze. Students should be encouraged to stay calm and ask for help if they need it.

For the second computer activity, students will access a minigame that can be made available in an alternative world on Minecraft® Realms, or engage in free play. Minigames are available to choose instead of a world template in any Realm. There are a variety of games to choose from; however, once chosen for the world, only the selected minigame will be available for other players.

KEY POINTS FOR DISCUSSION

- What kinds of problems might we face at home and school?
- How can we figure out what size a problem is? – refer to handout
- How can we match the size of the problem with the size of our reaction?
- How do others feel when our reaction does not match the size of the problem?

SKILLS TO HIGHLIGHT DURING THE SESSION

- Matching the size of the reaction to the size of the problem
- Problem solving
- Asking for and offering help
- Talking about shared interests

SIZE OF THE PROBLEM – SESSION PLAN

Time	Activity
5 min	Welcome
5 min	Review Group Rules and Home Challenge
10 min	Size of the Problem Talk as a group about the types of problems we might face at school and at home. Discuss how we can figure out what size a problem is based on how easy it is to solve.
5 min	Discuss today's activity - finding their way through a maze. What size problem would it be if they can't get out? What can they do to stay calm and keep trying?
10 min	Player 1 goes through maze
10 min	Player 2 goes through maze
5 min	Movement Break
10 min	Discuss our reactions to problems and how we need to match the size of our reaction to the size of the problem. How do others feel if our reaction doesn't match the size of the problem?
5 min	Talk as a group about the next activity – playing a minigame
10 min	Player 1 plays a minigame
10 min	Player 2 plays a minigame
5 min	Explain Home Challenge and Give Rewards
	Finish

SIZE OF THE PROBLEM

Today we learned how to work out the Size of a Problem and how to react appropriately during the following activities:

- With the group, we discussed the types of problems we might face at school and at home, and how to figure out what size a problem is based on how easy it is to solve.

- We practised matching our reaction to the size of the problem while navigating a maze on Minecraft® and playing some minigames with our partners.

- With the group we learned about appropriate reactions to different-sized problems, and how others feel when our reaction doesn't match the size of the problem.

SIZE OF THE PROBLEM

How big is the problem?

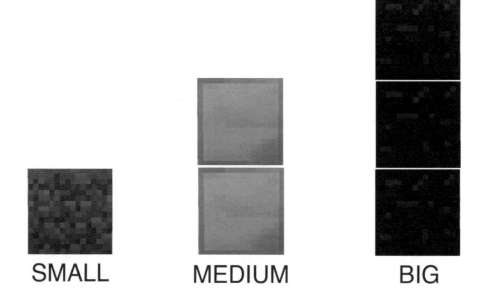

SMALL   MEDIUM   BIG

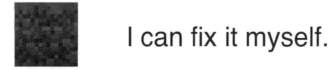 I can fix it myself.

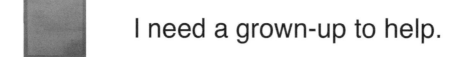 I need a grown-up to help.

 It's an emergency! Call for help!

How big is my reaction?

SMALL   MEDIUM   BIG

SIZE OF THE PROBLEM

Home Challenge

Sometimes when we have a problem, we think it is much bigger than it actually is and so our reaction doesn't match.

Think about a situation where your reaction didn't match the size of the problem.

What was the problem?

_____

_____

_____

How did you react?

_____

_____

If you had matched your reaction to the size of the problem, what would you have done?

_____

_____

_____

SESSION 23: BEING A GOOD SPORT

World set-up

In this session, the world needs to be flat or feature large open spaces, to enable students to create a pixel art trophy.

Computer activity

Students will create a pixel art trophy for their computer activity. Students may choose to create their own design, or copy one. It is recommended that an assortment of designs be downloaded and printed before the session and be made available to the students for ideas.

KEY POINTS FOR DISCUSSION

- What does it mean to be a 'good sport'? – refer to handout

- Why is it important to be a good sport when playing with others?

- What do bad sports do when they win or lose?

- How do bad sports make others feel?

- How should we react if someone is being a bad sport? – refer to handout

SKILLS TO HIGHLIGHT DURING THE SESSION

- Being a good sport when winning or losing games

- Using nice words

- Encouraging others

- Taking turns to talk

BEING A GOOD SPORT – SESSION PLAN

Time	Activity
5 min	Welcome
5 min	Review Home Challenge
10 min	Talk as a group about what it means to be a good sport. When is it important to be a Good Sport? (winning and losing) What does being a good sport look like? What do bad sports do when they win/lose? How does that make others feel?
5 min	Discuss today's activity – making a pixel art trophy
10 min	Player 1 builds a trophy (pixel art)
10 min	Player 1 builds a trophy (pixel art)
5 min	Movement Break
5 min	Play Minecraft® Snakes and Ladders with a partner
10 min	Discuss how we should react when someone is being a bad sport. Has anyone had that experience before? What should we do or say? Is it hard to stay calm?
10 min	Player 1 Free Play or board games
10 min	Player 2 Free Play or board games
5 min	Explain Home Challenge and Give Rewards
	Finish

BEING A GOOD SPORT

Today we learned about what being a Good Sport involves and why it is important, while completing the following activities:

o With the group, we discussed what a good sport does when they win or lose a game, and then what a bad sport might do and how that makes others feel.

o Working on the computers, we created a winner's trophy with pixel art. We also played some board games with our friends. We practised being good sports while playing together.

o With the group we discussed how we should react when someone we are playing with is being a bad sport (e.g. cheating, changing the rules, leaving the game before it is finished, getting angry, etc.).

BEING A GOOD SPORT

Play fair

Encourage others

Congratulate
the winners

1. Hands, feet and objects to yourself.
2. If you make it, you can break it.

Follow the rules

Be polite

Stay calm
if you lose

BEING A GOOD SPORT

What to do if someone is a bad sport:

1. Stay calm

2. Try to talk about the problem

3. Walk away

4. Ask an adult for help

BEING A GOOD SPORT

Home Challenge

Play the 'Minecraft® Snakes and Ladders' game with a family member or friend.

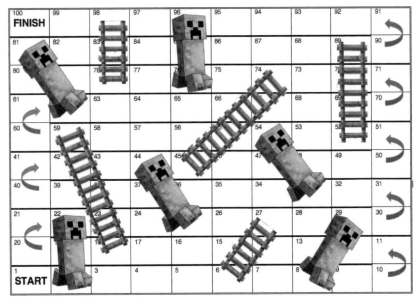

Remember to be a 'good sport' whether you win or lose.

How did you feel when you won/lost?

_____

What did you do at the end of the game to show you were a good sport?

_____

_____

SESSION 24: ACCEPTING CONSEQUENCES

World set-up

For this session, the world needs to have plenty of water in which to build underwater houses. An island or a location close to an ocean would be ideal.

Computer activity

In this session, students will design and build their own underwater houses. These can be built completely submerged in water, or breaching the surface, and can be created using any materials. It could be helpful to provide pictures of a few different underwater houses for students who are unsure of what an underwater house should look like.

KEY POINTS FOR DISCUSSION

· What are consequences? – refer to handout

· What are some examples of positive and negative consequences?

· When do negative consequences usually occur?

· Why is it important to consider consequences before we act?

· How can we take responsibility for our actions if we make the wrong choice? – refer to handout

SKILLS TO HIGHLIGHT DURING THE SESSION

· Being responsible

· Making good choices about behaviour

· Helping others

· Using nice words

ACCEPTING CONSEQUENCES – SESSION PLAN

Time	Activity
5 min	Welcome
5 min	Review Home Challenge
10 min	What are Consequences? Talk as a group about what consequences are. What are some examples of positive and negative consequences? When do negative consequences mostly occur?
5 min	Discuss today's activity – creating an underwater house. Talk with the group about what you need to consider before you start building. Discuss materials, placement, etc.
10 min	Player 1 builds an underwater house
10 min	Player 2 builds an underwater house
5 min	Movement Break
5 min	Discuss what features they have included in their underwater house with peers.
10 min	Why is it important and helpful to think about the consequences of behaviour before doing something? Why/how should we take responsibility for our behaviour?
10 min	Player 1 continues to build underwater house or Free Play
10 min	Player 2 continues to build underwater house or Free Play
5 min	Explain Home Challenge and Give Rewards
	Finish

ACCEPTING CONSEQUENCES

Today we explored how our behaviour can have positive and negative Consequences and the importance of taking responsibility for our behaviour during the following activities:

o With the group we discussed what consequences are, and the types of behaviour that can lead to positive or negative consequences.

o Working with partners, we designed and built underwater houses on the computers.

o With the group we discussed why it is important to think about the consequences of our behaviour before we do something, and be willing to accept the consequences of what we choose to do.

ACCEPTING CONSEQUENCES

What is a Consequence?

A consequence is the result or effect of a behaviour.

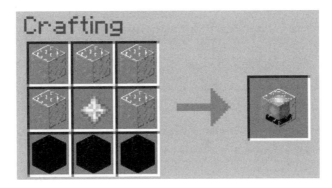

It is what happens after you do something.

A consequence can be positive or negative.

ACCEPTING CONSEQUENCES

How can we take responsibility for our behaviour?

1. Be honest about what you have done.

2. Don't make excuses or try to blame others.

3. Try and help solve the problem.

4. Explain yourself.

5. Calmly accept any consequences.

6. Let it go and move on.

ACCEPTING CONSEQUENCES

Home Challenge

Think about a situation where something might upset you.

Complete the flow chart below to show two actions you might take in response to the situation and the possible consequence of each.

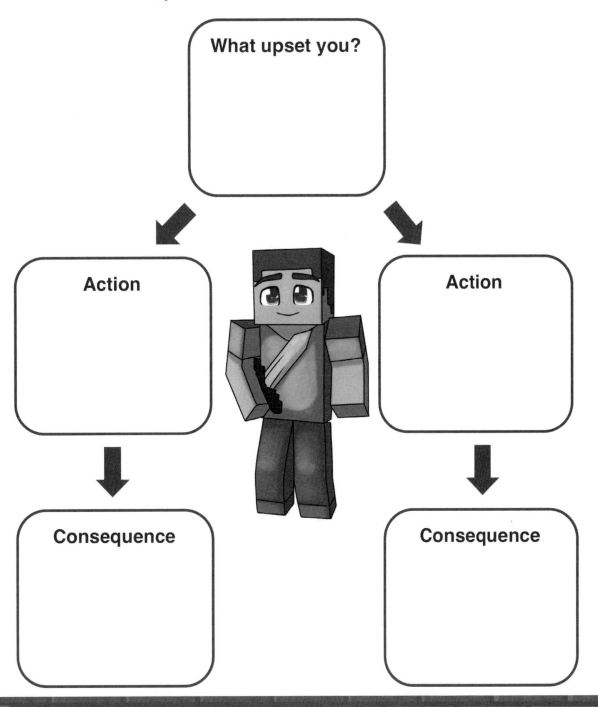

What upset you?

Action

Action

Consequence

Consequence

SESSION 25: PUTTING IT ALL TOGETHER – SUMMARY SESSION

World set-up

There are no specific requirements for the world for this session, as students can build their underground rollercoasters in any location. Ideally, a world with several different areas or landscapes would be best (e.g. flat area, forest, mountains).

Computer activity

In this session, students will build underground rollercoasters. They will need to find and adapt a cave or dig out a tunnel in the ground to create space to build their rollercoaster. Before going on the computers, the group should discuss the features that are important to include in their rollercoasters, and where they could be built.

To construct a rollercoaster, students will need standard rails, powered rails and a minecart from their inventory. Standard rails can be used for any downward parts of the rollercoaster and corners, and powered rails should be used when uphill movement is required.

KEY POINTS FOR DISCUSSION

- What is tone of voice?
- How can we figure out the size of a problem and an appropriate reaction?
- What does being a good sport look like?
- What is the difference between positive and negative consequences?

SKILLS TO HIGHLIGHT DURING THE SESSION

- Using an appropriate tone of voice when talking to our friends
- Matching the size of the reaction to the size of the problem
- Being a good sport
- Making a good choice about behaviour by thinking about consequences

---

PUTTING IT ALL TOGETHER – SESSION PLAN

Time	Activity
5 min	Welcome
5 min	Review Home Challenge
10 min	What have we learned about this week? ○ Tone of Voice ○ Size of the Problem ○ Being a Good Sport ○ Accepting Consequences Talk as a group about what we have learned and how we can use this information at school and at home.
5 min	Discuss today's activity – creating an underground rollercoaster. Talk with the group about finding a cave to start building. Discuss materials, placement, etc.
10 min	Player 1 builds an underground rollercoaster
10 min	Player 2 builds an underground rollercoaster
5 min	Movement Break
10 min	Discuss what they have created. Was it easy/hard? How did they use the skills they have learned this week?
10 min	Player 1 builds an underground rollercoaster or Free Play
10 min	Player 2 builds an underground rollercoaster or Free Play
10 min	Give Certificates and Rewards
	Finish

PUTTING IT ALL TOGETHER

Today we reviewed and practised the skills we have learned over the last few sessions during the following activities:

o With the group, we discussed what we have learned and how we can use these skills at home and at school.

o Working with partners, we made underground rollercoasters in Minecraft® and played some minigames. We had to:

- Use an appropriate TONE OF VOICE when talking to our partners
- Consider the SIZE OF THE PROBLEM if things didn't go to plan
- BE A GOOD SPORT whether we won or lost a game
- Think about the CONSEQUENCES of our actions and make good choices about our behaviour towards others.

SESSION 26: JOINING IN WITH OTHERS

World set-up

There are no specific requirements for the world for this session, as students can build their bridges in any location. Ideally, a world with several different areas or landscapes would be best (e.g. flat area, forest, mountains).

Computer activity

In this session, students will build bridges across the landscape out of any materials they choose from their inventory. It could be helpful to provide pictures of a few different types of bridges for students who are unsure of what a bridge should look like.

KEY POINTS FOR DISCUSSION

- When might you want to join in with others at home or school?

- How do we join in with a group? – refer to handout

- Has anyone ever said 'No' when you have tried to join a group?

- What can we do if someone says 'No'?

SKILLS TO HIGHLIGHT DURING THE SESSION

- Joining in with others

- Talking about shared interests

- Asking for and accepting help

- Using nice words

JOINING IN WITH OTHERS – SESSION PLAN

Time	Activity
5 min	Welcome and Introductions
10 min	Group Rules and Minecraft® Money
10 min	Joining In Talk as a group about when we might want to join in with others (e.g. a conversation, game, activity). How do we join in with a group?
5 min	Discuss today's activity – building a bridge. Work with partners to design a bridge, decide on materials etc.
10 min	Player 1 builds a bridge
10 min	Player 2 builds a bridge
5 min	Movement Break
10 min	How do we know when it is a good time to join in? What do we do if someone says no?
10 min	Player 1 Free Play (e.g. minigame, crafting, building, etc)
10 min	Player 2 Free Play (e.g. minigame, crafting, building, etc)
5 min	Explain Home Challenge and Give Rewards
	Finish

JOINING IN WITH OTHERS

Today we practised Joining In with others during the following activities:

o With the group, we discussed when we might want to join in with others and the five steps for joining in effectively.

o With our partners, we designed and built bridges across a river in Minecraft®.

o With the group, we practised joining in with our peers to play minigames on Minecraft® and participate in other activities.

JOINING IN WITH OTHERS

1. Move closer

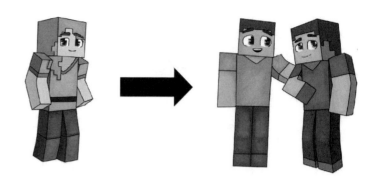

2. Look and listen

3. Think – is this a good time to join?

4. Greet others

5. Make a comment or ask a question

JOINING IN WITH OTHERS

Home Challenge

Think about a time when you tried to Join In with others.

Who were you trying to join?

_____

_____

What were they doing?

_____

_____

What did you do or say?

_____

_____

Were you allowed to join in?

_____

_____

How did you feel?

_____

_____

SESSION 27: RESPONDING TO TEASING

World set-up

In this session, the world needs to be flat or feature large open spaces, to enable students to create a giant water tank.

Computer activity

The activity for this session is building a giant fish tank. Students will need to use glass and other materials from their inventory to create a frame and the tank, then use a water bucket to fill the tank with water.

KEY POINTS FOR DISCUSSION

- What is teasing?

- How do you know if you are being teased?

- How can we tell if someone is teasing us to be mean or teasing in a friendly way? – refer to handout

- What can we do if we are being teased? – refer to handout

SKILLS TO HIGHLIGHT DURING THE SESSION

- Taking turns to talk

- Using kind words

- Helping others

RESPONDING TO TEASING – SESSION PLAN

Time	Activity
5 min	Welcome
5 min	Review Group Rules and Home Challenge
10 min	What is Teasing? Talk as a group about teasing – what it is, how to tell if someone is teasing you and what to do if you are being teased.
10 min	Discuss today's activity – building a giant fish tank. Talk with the group about what features it will need, what it should be made of, etc.
10 min	Player 1 builds a giant fish tank
10 min	Player 2 builds a giant fish tank
5 min	Movement Break
5 min	Discuss what features they have included in their fish tanks. What else would be good to add?
5 min	Talk as a group about their experiences of teasing. Have they been teased? Have they teased others? How does it feel to be teased?
10 min	Player 1 Free Play
10 min	Player 2 Free Play
5 min	Explain Home Challenge and Give Rewards
	Finish

RESPONDING TO TEASING

Today we learned about how to Respond to Teasing during the following activities:

o With the group, we discussed what teasing is, and how we can tell if someone is teasing in a friendly way or to be mean.

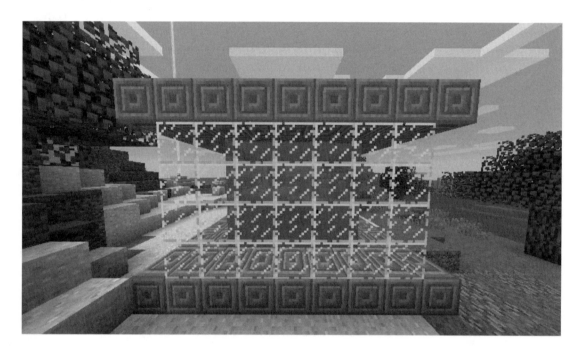

o Working with partners, we created giant fish tanks in Minecraft®. We had to consider what materials to use and what features to include.

o With the group, we talked about our experiences of being teased and what we can do if someone teases us.

RESPONDING TO TEASING

Friendly Teasing vs Mean Teasing

You can tell if someone is teasing you in a friendly or mean way by thinking about the following:

Is the person a friend or family member?

What tone of voice is the person using?

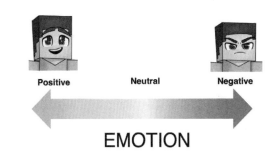

What does the person's body language tell you?

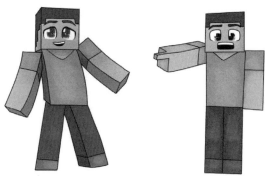

What past experiences have you had with the person?

RESPONDING TO TEASING

What can we do if we are being teased?

Accept the teasing

Make a joke

Walk away

Stand up for yourself

RESPONDING TO TEASING

Home Challenge

Imagine you are being teased in a friendly way by your brother. How would you respond?
(tick the strategies you would use)

Accept the teasing

Make a joke

Walk away

Stand up for yourself

Something else? _____

Now imagine you are being teased in a mean way by a bully at school. How would you respond?
(tick the strategies you would use)

Accept the teasing

Make a joke

Walk away

Stand up for yourself

Something else? _____

SESSION 28: MANAGING DIFFICULT FEELINGS

World set-up

For this session, you will need a desert world with flat ground so students can create a desert temple.

Computer activity

Students will build desert temples during this session. Before going on the computers, students will discuss the features of desert temples with the group, and then design their temple with partners. When they move to the computer, students can use any materials in their inventory to create their temple.

KEY POINTS FOR DISCUSSION

- What kinds of feelings are difficult to manage? – refer to handout

- How do we know when we are having those feelings?

- What makes us have difficult feelings?

- What can we do to feel better when we have difficult feelings? – refer to handout

SKILLS TO HIGHLIGHT DURING THE SESSION

- Staying calm

- Taking turns to talk

- Showing interest in others

- Using nice words

MANAGING DIFFICULT FEELINGS – SESSION PLAN

Time	Activity
5 min	Welcome
5 min	Review Home Challenge
10 min	Managing Difficult Feelings Talk as a group about what types of feelings are difficult to manage. How do we know we are having those feelings? What makes us feel that way?
10 min	Discuss today's activity – building a desert temple. Talk with the group about what materials they might use and what it might look like.
5 min	Design and plan a desert temple with partners
10 min	Player 1 builds a desert temple
10 min	Player 2 builds a desert temple
5 min	Movement Break
5 min	Discuss what we can do when we experience difficult feelings
10 min	Player 1 finishes desert temple or Free Play
10 min	Player 2 finishes desert temple or Free Play
5 min	Explain Home Challenge and Give Rewards
	Finish

MANAGING DIFFICULT FEELINGS

Today we explored how to recognize and Manage Difficult Feelings during the following activities:

o With the group, we discussed what difficult feelings are, when they occur and how we recognize them.

o On the computers, we worked with our partners to create desert temples in Minecraft®.

o As a group we discussed what we can do when we are having difficult feelings at school and at home, to help us feel better and make good choices about our behaviour.

MANAGING DIFFICULT FEELINGS

What are Difficult Feelings?

Difficult feelings make us feel uncomfortable or bad.

Anger

Frustration

Sadness

Fear

Worry

How do we recognize difficult feelings?

Thoughts

Actions

Physical reactions

MANAGING DIFFICULT FEELINGS

How do we manage Difficult Feelings effectively?

When you battle in Minecraft®, you have armour to protect you and tools to fight your enemy.

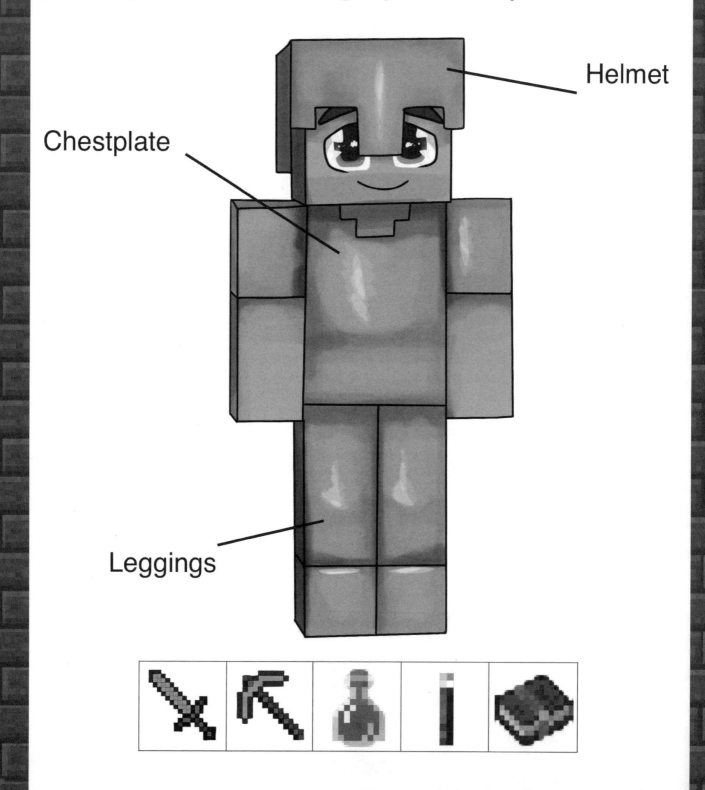

Helmet

Chestplate

Leggings

MANAGING DIFFICULT FEELINGS

How can you manage Difficult Feelings effectively?

When you have difficult feelings, you have no armour to protect you, so your feelings go to different parts of your body. You need tools to help you calm down and feel better.

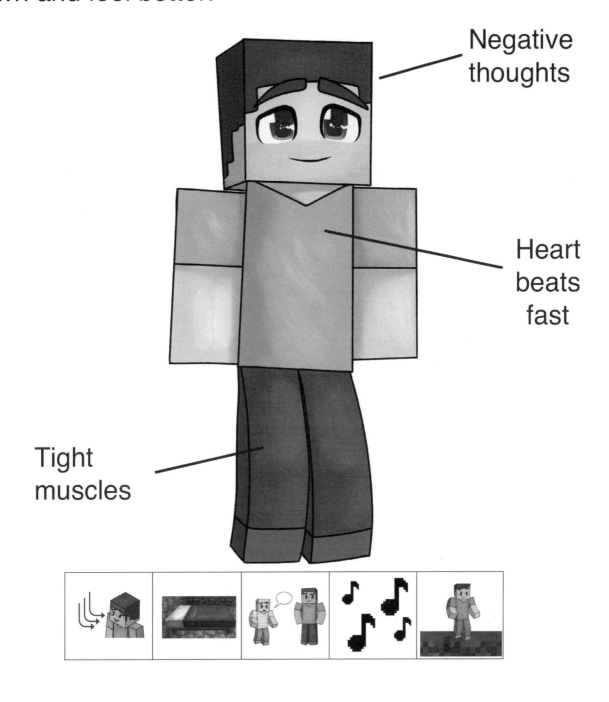

Negative thoughts

Heart beats fast

Tight muscles

MANAGING DIFFICULT FEELINGS

Home Challenge

Fill in the toolbar below to show what tools you use to feel better when you're angry (e.g. deep breaths, taking a break, asking for help, etc.).

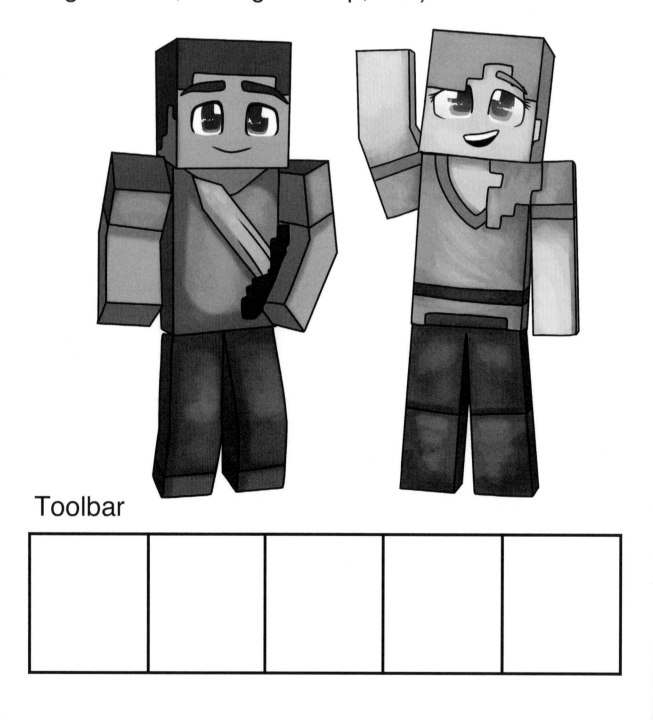

Toolbar

SESSION 29: BEING HONEST

World set-up

There are no specific requirements for the world for this session, as students can build their treehouses in any location. Ideally, a world with several different areas or landscapes would be best (e.g. flat area, forest, mountains).

Computer activity

In this session, students will design and build treehouses. As a group, students will discuss what materials to use and features to include in their treehouses. Then they will work on the computers in pairs to build their treehouses according to their design.

KEY POINTS FOR DISCUSSION

- What is honesty? – refer to handout

- Why is being honest important?

- Why might someone be dishonest or tell a lie?

- What happens when someone is dishonest/doesn't tell the truth?

SKILLS TO HIGHLIGHT DURING THE SESSION

- Helping others

- Telling the truth

- Taking turns to talk

- Using nice words

- Giving compliments

BEING HONEST – SESSION PLAN

Time	Activity
5 min	Welcome
5 min	Review Home Challenge
10 min	What is Honesty? Talk as a group about what honesty is and why it is important. What happens when we are dishonest/don't tell the truth?
10 min	Discuss today's activity – building a treehouse. Talk with the group about finding a place to build. Discuss materials, placement, furniture, etc.
10 min	Player 1 builds treehouse
10 min	Player 2 builds treehouse
5 min	Movement Break
10 min	Show treehouses to the group and discuss how they have been built.
10 min	Player 1 continues to build treehouse or Free Play
10 min	Player 2 continues to build treehouse or Free Play
5 min	Explain Home Challenge and Give Rewards
	Finish

BEING HONEST

Today we discussed why it is important to Be Honest during the following activities:

o With the group, we used examples to explore honesty and dishonesty, and discussed why we should always be honest with others.

o Working with partners, we built treehouses in Minecraft®. We had to design the treehouse, choose materials and find a good place to build.

o With the group, we discussed how we feel and how others feel when we are dishonest.

BEING HONEST

Say what really happened

Tell the whole truth

Do what is right

Be honest in your actions

BEING HONEST

Home Challenge

Think of a time when you were dishonest.

What were you dishonest about?

_____

_____

Why were you dishonest?

_____

_____

Did anyone find out you were being dishonest?

_____

_____

How did you feel?

_____

_____

What happened afterwards?

_____

_____

SESSION 30: PUTTING IT ALL TOGETHER – SUMMARY SESSION

World set-up

For this session, the world needs to have plenty of water in which to build pirate ships. An island or a location close to an ocean would be ideal.

Computer activity

In this session, students will design and build their own pirate ships. These can be built at the edge of the shore or in the water, and can be created using any materials. It could be helpful to provide pictures of a few different pirate ships for students who are unsure of what a pirate ship should look like.

KEY POINTS FOR DISCUSSION

- How can we join in effectively with others?

- What can we do if someone won't let us join in?

- How can we tell if someone is teasing to be mean or teasing in a friendly way?

- What can we do to feel better when we have difficult feelings?

- Why is it important to always be honest?

SKILLS TO HIGHLIGHT DURING THE SESSION

- Staying calm

- Telling the truth

- Talking about shared interests

- Helping others

PUTTING IT ALL TOGETHER – SESSION PLAN

Time	Activity
5 min	Welcome
5 min	Review Home Challenge
10 min	What have we learned about this week? ○ Joining In ○ Responding to Teasing ○ Managing Difficult Feelings ○ Being Honest Talk as a group about what we have learned and how we can use this information at school and at home.
10 min	Discuss today's activity – building a pirate ship. Decide in pairs what materials are needed, what it will look like, etc.
10 min	Player 1 builds a pirate ship
10 min	Player 2 builds a pirate ship
5 min	Movement Break
5 min	Discuss what they have created. Was it easy/hard? Show others what they have made.
10 min	Player 1 builds pirate ship or Free Play
10 min	Player 2 builds pirate ship or Free Play
10 min	Give Certificates and Rewards
	Finish

PUTTING IT ALL TOGETHER

Today we reviewed and practised the skills we have learned over the last few sessions during the following activities:

○ With the group, we discussed what we have learned and how we can use these skills at home and at school.

○ Working with partners, we made pirate ships in Minecraft® and played some minigames.

○ With the group we did a quiz to test our knowledge of the key themes from the last few sessions:
- JOINING IN
- RESPONDING TO TEASING
- MANAGING DIFFICULT FEELINGS
- BEING HONEST.

PART 3

RESOURCES

MINECRAFT® DOLLARS

MINECRAFT® SNAKES AND LADDERS

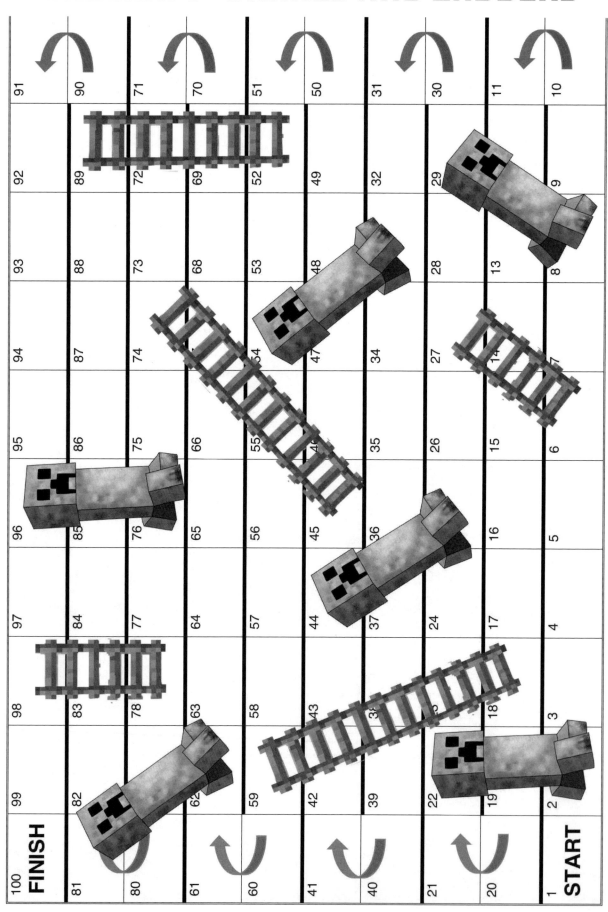

★

CONGRATULATIONS

THIS CERTIFICATE RECOGNIZES

_____

FOR SUCCESSFULLY COMPLETING THE

MINECRAFT® SOCIAL GROUP

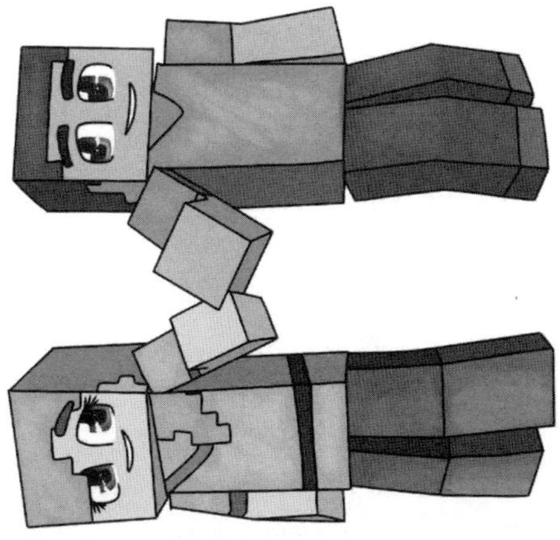

_____

PRESENTED BY: _____

DATE: _____

★

CONGRATULATIONS

THIS CERTIFICATE RECOGNIZES

FOR SUCCESSFULLY COMPLETING THE

MINECRAFT® SOCIAL GROUP

PRESENTED BY: _____

DATE: _____

CONGRATULATIONS

THIS CERTIFICATE RECOGNIZES

_____

FOR SUCCESSFULLY COMPLETING THE

MINECRAFT® SOCIAL GROUP

PRESENTED BY: _____

DATE: _____

HELPFUL WEBSITES

Minecraft® official website

https://minecraft.net

Minecraft® Wiki

https://minecraft.gamepedia.com

Minecraft® crafting recipes

www.minecraft-crafting.net

Minecraft® 101

www.minecraft101.net/index.html

BIBLIOGRAPHY

Anketell, C., Rose, R. (2009) The benefits of social skills groups for young people with autism spectrum disorder: A pilot study. *Child Care in Practice 15*, 2, 127–144.

Baron-Cohen, S., Gómez De La Cuesta, G., Krauss, G.W., LeGoff, D.B. (2014) *LEGO®-Based Therapy: How to Build Social Competence through LEGO®-based Clubs for Children with Autism and Related Conditions*. London: Jessica Kingsley Publishers.

Bernard-Opitz, V., Sriram, N., Nakhoda-Sapuan, S. (2001) Enhancing social problem solving in children with autism and normal children through computer-assisted instruction. *Journal of Autism and Developmental Disorders 31*, 4, 377–384.

Carpendale, J., Lewis, C. (2006) *How Children Develop Social Understanding*. Malden, MA: Blackwell Publishing.

Clifford Scheflen, C. (2009) *Video Modeling to Teach Play (Language and Social Skills) to Children with Autism*, presented at the US Autism & Asperger Association (USAAA) Conference, Los Angeles, CA., USA

Cook, J. (2011) *The Worst Day of My Life Ever!* Boys Town, NE: Boys Town Press.

Cook, J. (2012) *Sorry I Forgot to Ask!* Boys Town, NE: Boys Town Press.

Cook, J. (2012) *Team Work Isn't My Thing and I Don't Like to Share!* Boys Town, NE: Boys Town Press.

Cook, J. (2013) *I Just Want to Do It My Way!* Boys Town, NE: Boys Town Press.

Cook, J. (2013) *Thanks for the Feedback, I Think.* Boys Town, NE: Boys Town Press.

Cook, J. (2014) *I Can't Believe You Said That!* Boys Town, NE: Boys Town Press.

Cook, J. (2015) *But It's Not My Fault!* Boys Town, NE: Boys Town Press.

Cook, J. (2016) *That Rule Doesn't Apply to Me!* Boys Town, NE: Boys Town Press.

Cordeiro, A., Nelson, E. (2015) *Minecraft® Construction for Dummies®, Portable Edition*. Hoboken, NJ: John Wiley & Sons Inc.

Cordeiro, J. (2015) *Minecraft® Redstone for Dummies®, Portable Edition*. Hoboken, NJ: John Wiley & Sons Inc.

Dekker, V., Nauta, M.H., Mulder, E.J., Timmerman, M.E., de Bildt, A. (2014) A randomized controlled study of a social skills training for preadolescent children with autism spectrum disorders: Generalization of skills by training parents and teachers? *BMC Psychiatry 14*, 189. Retrieved from: www.biomedcentral.com/1471-244X/14/189 (accessed 18 June 2018).

Delsandro, E. (2013) *Practical Strategies for Using Video Modeling for Teaching Social Skills to Children with Autism*. Rockville, MD: Model Me Kids. Retrieved from: www.modelmekids.com/workshop/powerpoint%20Liz%20Delsandro.pdf (accessed 18 June 2018).

Farwell, N. (2015) *Minecraft: Redstone Handbook (Updated Edition): An Official Mojang Book*. New York, NY: Scholastic Inc.

Franzone, E., Collet-Klingenberg, L. (2008) *Overview of Video Modeling*. Madison, WI: The National Professional Development Center on Autism Spectrum Disorders, Waisman Center, University of Wisconsin.

Graves, S. (2012) *Hippo Owns Up*. London: Franklin Watts.

Graves, S. (2016) *Elephant Learns to Share*. London: Windmill Books.

Graves, S. (2016) *Monkey Needs to Listen*. London: Franklin Watts.

Harper, C.B., Symon, J.B.G., Frea, W.D. (2008) Recess is time-in: Using peers to improve social skills of children with autism. *Journal of Autism and Developmental Disorders 38*, 5, 815–826.

Jones, S., Brush, K., Bailey, R., Brion-Meisels, G., *et al.* (2017) *Navigating SEL from the Inside Out: Looking Inside & Across 25 Leading SEL Programs: A Practical Resource for Schools and OST Providers*. Cambridge, MA: Harvard Graduate School of Education. Retrieved from: www.wallacefoundation.org/knowledge-center/Documents/Navigating-Social-and-Emotional-Learning-from-the-Inside-Out.pdf (accessed 18 June 2018).

Kasari, C., Rotheram-Fuller, E., Locke, J., Gulsrud, A. (2012) Making the connection: Randomized controlled trial of social skills at school for children with autism spectrum disorders. *Journal of Child Psychology and Psychiatry 53*, 4, 431–439.

Koegel, R.L., Kern Koegel, L., Oliver, K. (2016) Using a child's restricted interests to increase social inclusion. *The Oracle: Organization for Autism Research*. Retrieved from: https://researchautism.org/using-a-childs-restricted-interest-to-increase-social-inclusion (accessed 18 June 2018).

LeGroff, D.B. (2017) *How LEGO®-Based Therapy for Autism Works: Landing on My Planet*. London: Jessica Kingsley Publishers.

Meadows, C. (2017) *Understanding Child Development: Psychological Perspectives and Applications*. Abingdon: Taylor & Francis Ltd.

Mojang, A.B. (2015) *Minecraft: Beginner's Handbook (Updated Edition): An Official Minecraft Book from Mojang*. London: Egmont UK Ltd.

Mojang, A.B. (2017) *Minecraft Guide to Creative: An Official Minecraft Book from Mojang*. London: Egmont Childrens Books.

Mulchay, W. (2012) *Zach Apologizes*. Minneapolis, MN: Free Spirit Publishing.

Mulchay, W. (2012) *Zach Gets Frustrated*. Minneapolis, MN: Free Spirit Publishing.

Mulchay, W. (2016) *Zach Makes Mistakes*. Minneapolis, MN: Free Spirit Publishing.

Mulchay, W. (2017) *Zach Hangs In There*. Minneapolis, MN: Free Spirit Publishing.

Needler, M., Southam, P. (2015) *Minecraft: Construction Handbook (Updated Edition): An Official Mojang Book*. New York, NY: Scholastic Inc.

Ratcliffe, B., Wong, M., Dossetor, D., Hayes, S. (2014) Teaching social-emotional skills to school-aged children with autism spectrum disorder: A treatment versus control trial in 41 mainstream schools. *Research in Autism Spectrum Disorders 8*, 12, 1722–1733.

Reichow, B., Steiner, A.M., Volkmar, F. (2012) Social skills groups for people aged 6 to 21 with autism spectrum disorders (ASD). *Cochrane Database of Systematic Reviews*, 7, doi: 10.1002/14651858. CD008511.pub2.

Shapiro, L.E. (2004) *101 Ways to Teach Children Social Skills: A Ready-to-Use Reproducible Activity Book.* Farmingville, NY: Bureau for At-Risk Youth.

Smith, B. (2015) *If Winning Isn't Everything, Why Do I Hate to Lose?* Boys Town, NE: Boys Town Press.

Smith, B. (2016) *My Day Is Ruined!* Boys Town, NE: Boys Town Press.

Smith, B. (2016) *What Were You Thinking!* Boys Town, NE: Boys Town Press.

Smith, B. (2017) *Of Course It's a Big Deal!* Boys Town, NE: Boys Town Press.

Smith Myles, B., Southwick, J. (2005) *Asperger Syndrome and Difficult Moments: Practical Solutions for Tantrums, Rage, and Meltdowns* (second edition). Shawnee, KS: Autism Asperger Publishing Co.

Walker, S., Berthelsen, D.C. (2007) The social participation of young children with developmental disabilities in inclusive early childhood programs. *Electronic Journal for Inclusive Education* 2(2).

Williams, C., Wright, B. (2004) *How to Live with Autism and Asperger Syndrome: Practical Strategies for Parents and Professionals.* London: Jessica Kingsley Publishers.

Wong, C., Odom, S.L., Hume, K.A., Cox, A.W., *et al.* (2015) Evidence-based practices for children, youth, and young adults with autism spectrum disorder: A comprehensive review. *Journal of Autism and Developmental Disorders 45*, 7, 1951–1966.

INDEX OF HANDOUTS